The most definitive study of real success in print today. By reading and understanding these truths, you can live them.

—Larry Wilson
Author of *Changing the Game: The New Way to Sell*

Denis Waitley never fails to open fresh vistas on the subject of human achievement. . . . He deftly exposes phony views of success, tells how to overcome setbacks, how to find self-esteem, and how to apply his practical approach to setting goals. The Waitley way works, as his own career amply proves, and *Being the Best* should make just about anybody better.

—W. Clement Stone
Chairman of Aon Corporation and
Chairman of W. Clement Stone PMA Communications

Dr. Waitley's reflective, amusing, and authoritative book is a MUST for anyone wanting to find success within themselves. In this valuable book, we can see how Dr. Waitley and others became the best they can be and realize WE CAN TOO!

—Lee F. Hardy
President, Teli USA

Denis Waitley puts into "concrete" a philosophy in which I have always believed—and that is to *be* the very best *YOU* that you can become. God did not have time to make a nobody—just a somebody. The seeds of greatness are planted in every human being, and it is up to you—and to me—to bring them into fruition.

—Mary Kay Ash
Chairman of the Board, Mary Kay Cosmetics

Being the Best is a most needed book in the U.S. today. It cuts through the "success jungle" to reinstate integrity and inner affirmation as the driving force and only hope for the future of America. A must for every person whose desire is not just to reach the top by any available means, but to serve with integrity and personal satisfaction on whatever level of the success ladder.

> —Lars B. Dunberg
> International Executive Director
> Living Bibles International

Denis Waitley is among *the best* in teaching principles of living successfully. *Being the Best* adds immeasurably to his stature as an author and a psychologist.

> —Robert H. Schuller
> Founding Pastor, Crystal Cathedral and Hour of Power

. . . a refresher course of the good things my parents told me about self-discipline, good habits, and finding my natural gifts. Perfect reading for anyone interested in finding realistic success, not some phony, materialistic, ego-stroking substitute.

> —J. David Schmidt
> Author and Marketing Consultant

. . . clearly shows the way toward *Being the Best*. Reading it does three things for me: (1) inspires me to be and do better; (2) makes me believe I can not only be better, but that I can be my best; (3) shows me the pathway.

> —Charles L. Allen
> Minister, Retired, First United Methodist Church
> Houston, Texas

. . . . Denis Waitley shows us, most graphically, the difference between the mythical superficial success, and the genuine article. It's important that we know the difference. It's important that we know that genuine success can be an important part of all our lives.

> —Earl Nightingale
> Author and Radio Commentator

Being the Best is a collection of thoughts and principles, some new and some not so new, presented in a way that makes sense. The attention-getting, and keeping, style of Waitley's writing allows readers to actually see parallels to their own lives and how they, too, can be the best—no matter who they are or what they do!

> —Nanci Mason
> Former National Vice President, Future Farmers of America

Success is a decision. Denis Waitley's *Being the Best* will help anyone live a more successful, more productive life.

> —Dexter R. Yager, Sr.
> Crown Direct, Amway

BEING THE BEST

BEING THE BEST

DENIS WAITLEY

OLIVER
NELSON

A Division of Thomas Nelson Publishers

Nashville

Published in Nashville, Tennessee, by Oliver-Nelson Books, a division of Thomas Nelson, Inc., Publishers, and distributed in Canada by Lawson Falle, Ltd., Cambridge, Ontario.

The Bible verses used in this publication are from THE NEW KING JAMES VERSION. Copyright © 1979, 1980, 1982, Thomas Nelson, Inc., Publishers.

In chapter 3, the ethics test by William D. Brown is reprinted from PMA Adviser (September 1986) 5:9 and is used with permission.

The poem at the end of chapter 8 is reprinted with permission of the Reader's Digest and Dorothy Heller.

Printed in the United States of America.

Library of Congress Cataloging-in-Publication Data

Waitley, Denis.
  Being the best.

  Bibliography: p.
  1. Success. I. Title.
BJ1611.2.W26 1987   158'.1   87–20363
ISBN 0-8407-9071-6

1   2   3   4   5   6   7   8—92   91   90   89   88   87

To Debbie, Dayna, Denis, Darren, Kim, and Lisa.

I'm so proud God chose me to have you as children.
Along with Susan, my beloved wife,
you are the "Best"
and most priceless treasures that I cherish.
Your lives are my celebration!

CONTENTS

9 PASSION, PRACTICE, AND PERSEVERANCE

Nothing happens without self-discipline • Setting priorities is as easy as A-B-C • The anatomy of a habit • Your RAS accepts negative or positive input • My RAS became a "boataholic" • Don't break your bad habits—replace them • Practice, then practice some more • Self-discipline does within while you do without • Learning from Littler's picture-perfect golf swing • Why some of the most talented never make it • Self-discipline takes time—and more time • Move from also-ran to winner's circle

10 TURNING FAILURE INTO FERTILIZER

Success is "in" at the Library of Congress • Totally avoiding failure means doing nothing • The story of Domino's Pizza • Never identify yourself with your failures • What happens when you really foul up? • Practical versus neurotic perfectionism • Focusing in a totaled 240Z • When disappointed . . . persevere! • Fear and failure are first cousins • Nothing is certain but death, taxes—and change • Are you as smart as a bee or a mouse?

11 A FIVE-STAR RATING

Graciousness is not gracious living • Do you know who you really are? • America's richest man is a true success • Do you appreciate what you really have? • "Baseball . . . gave me everything" • Are you living at the right pace for you? • Do you go that extra mile—every day? • A little difference makes the big difference

ACKNOWLEDGMENTS

This work represents the best of me. It would still be an unwritten and unpublished song in my heart and soul and head if I had not been blessed with the finest team of professionals and friends to put ideas and experiences into book form.

These special people and many more are the real artists:

Sam Moore, a publisher with great vision, resource, and faith.

Victor Oliver, a creative genius with boundless energy and a true friend.

Fritz Ridenour, an outstanding writer, alter ego, buddy, and the real maestro in making my best efforts much better. Thank you for always exceeding expectations.

Lila Empson, a fine editor and a joy to work with, even "under the gun."

Bruce Barbour, Sara Fortenberry, Paul Shepherd, and all their team members who, in the final analysis, gave this author his best opportunity to be read.

WITH A NAME LIKE "DUMBO," YOU'VE GOT TO BE GOOD

YOU MIGHT SAY I had a mythical childhood. What few fantasies radio didn't inspire, storybook characters from my weekly binge at the public library did. When I look back to the 1930s, 1940s, and early 1950s, I realize that my dog-eared orange library card was more valuable to me then than my slick orange-and-gold MasterCard is to me now. It didn't matter if the books were fiction or nonfiction. All of them were passports to faraway places and wonderful adventures.

All my life I have been fascinated by the mysterious relationship between myth and truth. As children, we regularly mix myths and truths. This is of no real concern unless we carry forward and cling to the myths in the arena of real living. For many of us, the myths slip in as facts, and before we know it, we have been sold a bill of goods that leads us down a worthless, frustrating dead-end road.

Like that of most kids of my generation, my fantasy world centered on the radio, the library and, of course, Saturdays at the Roxy Theatre. When I could earn the dime for a ticket and the extra two nickels for popcorn and a soft drink, the silver screen became a prime spawning ground for my still-boundless imagination.

I did a lot of pretending when I was growing up. My comic book collection helped me pretend I was the "Green Lantern," "Hawkman," and "The Blue Beetle" all rolled into one undersized kid. I pretended my father didn't have to go away to war. I pretended my mom and dad got along better and they didn't always have financial problems.

I was born and raised in San Diego, California, during the post-depression and World War II years. Like many of my friends, I recall cutting out pieces of cardboard and slipping them inside my shoes each morning so I wouldn't wear holes through my socks. What a pair of shoes mine were! They were my school shoes, gym shoes, and Sunday shoes all in one pair, and I took good care of them knowing that they had to last at least a year or until my feet outgrew them.

CHICKEN SANDWICHES WITHOUT THE CHICKEN

We had little money, but my mom was ingenious in making us seem rich. She packed my lunch, usually a sandwich and an apple, as if it were a gourmet express, takeout delicacy. I remember the morning I asked her what the sandwich-of-the-day was, expecting her usual answer of "peanut butter and something." She answered, with a twinkle in her eye, "Why, today you're getting a delicious chicken sandwich . . . without the chicken!"

And so I did. My chicken sandwich without the chicken was two pieces of Wonder bread with Nucoa margarine, lettuce, salt, pepper, and mayonnaise between them. My mom could even make poverty fun!

MY WISE FATHER

My dad also had a keen imagination, and we would often play a little good-night game that became our special ritual. He would come into my room to talk to me and listen to the triumphs and tragedies of my day. As he was leaving, Dad had a way of leaning back against the switch by my door and rubbing against it to "magically" blow out my light like the birthday candles on a cake.

As he did his little routine, Dad would say: "I'm blowing out your light now, and it will be dark for you. In fact, as far as you're concerned, it will be dark all over the world because the only world you ever know is the one you see through your own eyes. So remember, Son, keep your light bright. The world is yours to see that way. I love you, Son. Good night."

When I was very young, I used to lie there in bed after Dad left and try to understand what he meant. It was confusing to think that the whole world was dark when I was asleep and that the only world I would ever know was the one I would see through my own eyes. What Dad was trying to tell me was that when I went to sleep at night, as far as I was concerned, the world came to a stop. When I woke up in the morning, I could choose to see a fresh new world through my own eyes—if I kept my light bright. In other words, if I woke up happy, the world was happy. If I woke up not feeling well, the world was not as well off.

A LIFE-CHANGING LESSON FROM MY FATHER

My father's guidance about self-perception and the power in the eye of the beholder was invaluable. What he was trying to teach me with his little light show was this: "Denis, everything depends on how you want to look at what happens in life. It doesn't make any difference what is going on 'out there'—What makes a difference is how you take it."

Instead of teaching me "my glass was half-empty," my father taught me "my glass was more than half-full." He taught me to view life as something that was continually opening and expanding with new opportunities and events to enjoy.

Somewhere he picked up a bit of quantum physics theory. Depending on the kind of experiment you conduct, a particle of light can become a light beam or a light wave. It all depends on how you want to examine it. The light can change form, not because of its properties—it still remains light—but because of how you choose to behold it. My dad taught me that ugliness or beauty is in the eye of the beholder. Want and abundance are in the eye of the beholder. Being mediocre or being the best depends on the eye of the beholder.

Those good-night rituals with my father taught me that it didn't make any difference what the other kids said, what the other kids wore, or what they did. Their opinion of me wasn't that important. What was important was the way I handled what they might do and say.

Because I was so busy enjoying library books, favorite radio programs, the Saturday matinee, plus school, sports, friends, and especially my family, I don't ever remember wishing we were rich and famous. Picking up a few nickels and dimes running errands or mowing lawns kept me as rich as I thought I needed to be. I know my older sister, Diane, and my younger brother, Damon, felt the same way.

Meanwhile, I was discovering those gems of truth and wisdom buried in some of the myths and fantasies that came my way. Possibly the greatest converter of myth to truth the world has ever seen was Walt Disney. In particular, I learned a lot from Disney's lovable character, Dumbo, the pachyderm with the hang-glider ears.

When the movie was released in our town in 1943, I squirmed in my seat like any other ten-year-old with open-mouthed anguish as I watched poor Dumbo plunging toward disaster because he had dropped the "magic feather" that had empowered him to fly! When Dumbo pulled out of that deadly dive under his own ear power, I almost jumped to my feet and cheered. Dumbo didn't need that feather at all!

Whatever the plot was supposed to convey, my interpretation was, "You gotta have faith." When you believe, your faith gives you the power to do what you have to do in time of need. If Dumbo could find the courage to fly on his own and put on his own solo elephant Blue Angels air show, what might I be able to do when the time came?

THE CROWNING OF "DUMBO" WAITLEY

I remember as if it were yesterday seeing that movie *Dumbo* on the weekend, and on Monday back at school Dale Michael, the class bully, flicked my outsized ears with a wooden ruler and measured them. Then he proclaimed to the rest of the sixth-grade class that henceforth I was to be known as "Dumbo" Waitley, the kid with the biggest ears in Pacific Beach Grammar School.

The other kids cheered at first, then they jeered. Like Dumbo's magic feather, my fragile ten-year-old self-image fluttered to ground zero. The name "Dumbo" stuck with me for the next seven years until I got out of La Jolla High in 1950.

It doesn't make any difference what is going on "out there"—what makes a difference is how you take it

---

✻

But along the way, I kept discovering truths among all the slings, arrows, and myths. My grandma read to me from the Good Book and taught me the golden rule and a faith that went beyond flying elephants. How I loved that precious, inspiring and gracious lady, my grandma! She taught me that no matter how cruel kids were to me, I should always treat everybody in the way I most wanted to be treated. And so, I always have.

I learned that failings and shortcomings can be changed from stumbling blocks into stepping stones. I remembered what Dad taught me about the light and the eye of the beholder and that what mattered wasn't what came into my life but how I handled it. I decided to capitalize on my nickname. If I were to be known by such a name, I'd put that name in lights. With a name like "Dumbo," you'd better be good. So I decided to set an example as a straight A student, athlete, and citizen.

"That's it," I reasoned. "I'll turn failure into fertilizer and use it to grow!"

I found that I didn't need a magic feather or any other kind of magical help. I went on to win varsity letters and get straight A's in high school. It took faith, knowledge, and hours of extra study. It took discipline and persistence and a strong inner value system that I got from my dad, my grandma, and my mother to insulate me against the rising heat of peer pressure.

In my senior year I ran for student body president, and my campaign slogans included these:

"Don't be dumb, vote for Dumbo."

"An elephant never forgets (his campaign promises)."

"Make La Jolla High fly with Dumbo."

How sweet it was to graduate from high school an honor student, varsity letterman, and student body president in an average, undersized body from a family with below-average income while still possessing those above-average ears!

PINOCCHIO GOES TO ANNAPOLIS

I recall another mythical Disney character who taught me truths I have used all my life. As I graduated from high school and won an appointment to Annapolis at the outbreak of the Korean War, I felt like Pinocchio, the wooden puppet who lost his strings and became "alive." Just as Pinocchio did, I became cocky and self-assured. If I could rise from the ignominy of being called Dumbo and become one of the chosen few to wear the blue and gold of a midshipman at Annapolis, did I have any limits at all?

I left for the Naval Academy believing I had no limits whatsoever. If I could conceive it and believe it, why couldn't I achieve it? I had worked my way through and paid my dues. I was a "success," and it would be all downhill from here.

Just like Pinocchio who looked for shortcuts, expediency, and immediate gratification, I expected to breeze through Annapolis with a 4.0 and go on to captain my own aircraft carrier. If you recall Disney's film, Pinocchio exaggerated his own importance, stretched the truth, and thereby sprouted a nose with a built-in bird's nest. He fell in with bad companions, journeyed to Pleasure Island, had a ball with self-indulgence, turned into a jackass, got swallowed by Monstro the Whale, was reunited with his father, discovered integrity, and finally became a real boy.

My career in the Naval Academy had some interesting parallels. I arrived with an exaggerated sense of self-importance and ability, looked for the path of least resistance, and never found it. I tried to PR my way through and nearly flunked out. Finally, I recognized the jackass that kept looking back at me from the mirror, swallowed my pride, decided to make a whale of an effort, uncovered my integrity, and became a real midshipman.

In my junior year at Annapolis I knuckled down, studied, marched, sang in the Chancellor Choir, participated in sports, and traded away all my childhood myths and fantasies for a commitment to live and seek the truth. For more than thirty years, I have been studying, learning, and teaching principles of how to be a successful human being.

I'D LIKE TO BE YOUR JIMINY CRICKET

A remnant of my childhood myths I don't mind carrying at all is that many people call me their personal Jiminy Cricket, the voice in their ear that urges them to follow their conscience, seek the truth, and never give up trying to reach their goals. And, of course, at my thirty-fifth high-school reunion, they still called me Dumbo.

My search for answers for what makes human beings fruitful and fulfilled continued in earnest after I got out of Annapolis in 1955 and went on to flight school at Pensacola to become a navy pilot. How I moved from there to the world of corporate consultation, fund raiser for the Salk Institute for Biological Studies (founded by Dr. Jonas Salk), and finally professional speaker, author, and seminar leader is a story I'll share in chapters 6 and 7.

I recorded the audiocassette program "The Psychology of Winning" in

1978, and it has become the best-selling personal growth program of its kind in the world. Thanks to my publisher, The Nightingale-Conant Corporation, the success of this program has provided opportunities for me beyond my greatest expectations. From the halls of Congress to Carnegie Hall, from the opera house in Sydney, Australia, to parliament houses in Europe, from the board rooms of corporate executives to the locker rooms of Olympic athletes, from the classrooms of primary and secondary schools to the living rooms of middle-class Americans, my mission has always been the same: to shatter the myths of cheap success and teach the eternal truths about what it really takes to make the most out of life.

Please note I said "*make* the most," not "*take* the most." There is a *big* difference, and that difference is what this book is all about. This book can help you, your family, your fellow workers, and your friends explore two critical questions:

> Are you takers who hope life will be good to you if you are smart enough, tough enough, ambitious enough, and lucky enough?

OR

> Are you makers who get the most out of life by giving the best you have and being the best you can be?

One question embodies myth; the other frames lasting truth. The key is always to be able to tell the myth from the truth in the game of life where the clock is always running and there are no time-outs. If you're game to get started, turn the page.

CHAPTER 1

EXPOSING THE SUCCESS MYTHS

MY TALKING ABOUT exposing the success myths may sound as if I'm down on the idea of succeeding, but that's not true. Indeed, I believe in living life to the hilt every day. And what's the purpose of living life unless one strives to be successful?

I don't believe success is something to be possessed, however. Rather, it is the process of becoming all I can and should be. Who among us has not cheered on Mother Teresa as she strives step by step to heal the hurts of the down-and-outers in Calcutta? We must remember that success has little to do with money, although there is nothing wrong with being a rich success. Some rich people are extremely successful; others are not.

Success has little to do with your personal "score" in life, although there is nothing wrong with putting plenty of points on the board when you can do it fair and square. Beware, however, of the idea that to be a real success you must outscore everyone else. If you measure your success only by what you purchase or produce, you are doomed to eternal dissatisfaction. There is always someone who can purchase or produce faster or better. There is always someone prettier, more popular, quicker, smarter, stronger. Whatever you use for your measuring stick, success is always just beyond your fingertips.

Why, then, title this book *Being the Best*? What does it mean to be the best? This is a strong value statement. It implies that there are criteria that can help us identify if we are being successful or not. I can say one thing for sure. Many of the traditional values and life principles that have always been associated with success, such as truth, morality, and integrity, have been rejected and obscured and overlaid with the myths of a value system interested only in self-gratification. The success myths saturate our every waking moment. Here are some examples:

- You can have it all, baby
- No one ever remembers who came in second.
- If you've got it, flaunt it!
- Winning is everything. In fact, it's the *only thing*.

You always project on the outside how you feel on the inside

✳

Television and other seductive media program us to believe that in whatever arena of life we find ourselves, being the best means there is some kind of standard out there that all of us must reach if we want to be winners. They tell us life is like a big game show, and the prizes we should all shoot for include the following:

- Instant name recognition
- Wealth
- Constant happiness
- On-going youthful vitality and beauty
- The special #1 image

This mythical standard of success is spreading like a cancer through the very fibers of our culture. We need only to look at the preoccupation with material wealth to realize that we are in real danger. But the ads don't tell us we can't drink, inhale, or snort happiness. We can't buy happiness, wear it, drive it, live in it, or travel to it! Happiness is the journey, not the destination. Happiness is rooted in the inner life, the being and living of life—not the outer trappings, the items we own and acquire, the positions and kudos we achieve and receive.

What good are fortune and fame if we miss the really valuable things such as love, family, friends, respect, and health, to name only a few? As one well-to-do invalid was heard to say, "There is nothing special about using a gold bed pan. I'd gladly trade all my annuities for two more healthy years of life."

Excellence in any endeavor is a worthy goal to pursue, but the artificial standard of success that is currently dangled before our media-mesmerized eyes reminds me of the sweet singing of the mythical creatures known as sirens. As ships approached their island, the sirens' song was at first beguiling, then irresistible, as it filled the ears of the unwary sailors who were eventually lured to their doom.

I am thoroughly convinced that unless our society takes a new, hard look at what success is all about, we can face the same kind of fate. Perhaps talking about being lured to one's doom sounds out of place for a behavioral scientist who has taught thousands of people about positive self-image, positive self-expectancy, and positive self-awareness over the past thirty years. I will have to take that chance because I am suffering from positive self-alarm, and I want to warn as well as help two major groups of readers.

The first group may be just starting out, itching to learn more about success and how to achieve it. If you're in this category, you want good advice because you're not interested in detours that lead to frustration or delays in your climb up the ladder of accomplishment.

Or perhaps you fit into the second group, which has been around quite a bit longer. You have tried all the self-help books, listened to the cassettes, watched the training videos, and attended the seminars. You have tried it all, and the pot of gold is still out there somewhere at the end of one of Murphy's laws:

NOTHING EVER QUITE WORKS OUT

Or to paraphrase Murphy, nothing ever quite works the way the success gurus say it will.

Even having it all doesn't necessarily satisfy. Ironically enough, disillusionment is occurring in the ranks of the much-publicized and much-glamorized Yuppies (young urban professionals) who are discovering that a high-paying job can be long on salary but short on satisfaction. Douglas LaBier, a psychologist who studied the Yuppies generation for almost ten years, has written a book about their angst, appropriately entitled *Modern Madness: The Emotional Fallout of Success*.

It seems that more than a few Yuppies are finding that they can stuff their Victorian houses with antiques and high-tech gadgetry, but they still wind up feeling empty inside. One thirty-nine-year-old lawyer was earning a lot of money but working long hours at what she felt was excruciatingly boring and meaningless activity. She complained to her superior who tried to help her understand. The very nature of their work was *supposed* to be boring and meaningless. In fact, it had no social usefulness, but for that they were "handsomely rewarded."[1]

Many Yuppies are discovering that there is more to life than money. Life must have meaning. They are descendants of the Yippies, the rebels of the sixties and seventies who many in the Establishment might label young insolent punks. But at least the Yippies thought they had a cause. All of their ruckus raising had some meaning because they were fighting for ideals, however distorted and counterproductive many of their practices were.

Disillusioned as the Yuppies may be, it is quite possible that they will soon be surpassed in feelings of meaninglessness and depression by a new group that has been labeled the DINKS (*D*ouble *I*ncome, *N*o *K*ids). These are the Yuppies who have decided that having it all includes not sharing it with any children. They are having too much fun making money, spending it, and experiencing life.

And beyond the DINKS are still more subgroups clamoring for recognition. I've already heard of

- The OINKS—*O*ne *I*ncome, *N*o *K*ids
- The SINKAS—*S*ingle *I*ncome, *N*o *K*ids Anymore
- The DIPS—*D*ual *I*ncome, *P*aying *S*upport

These tongue-in-cheek labels reflect the same desire that is deep within all of us. I like Rabbi Kushner's thoughts in his new book, *When All You've Ever Wanted Isn't Enough*. Just ask people what they want out of life, and the answer will usually center on something like this: "All I want is to be happy." Kushner observes that we all work very hard at making ourselves happy. We buy books, take courses, and try different lifestyles, but in the long run we do not feel that happy.

Kushner wonders about why happiness is so elusive. Why should people—like the Yuppies—with so many reasons to be happy feel that there is something missing? Are we asking for too much when we ask for happiness? Is it a goal that will remain forever out of reach? Or is it possible to be happy if we go at it the right way?[2]

Because I've been labeled by some as one of those success gurus who is supposed to know about how to be happy, I think it's time I leveled with you about the meaning of being the best. After all, what could make one happier than being the best?

In *Seeds of Greatness*, I shared the ten best-kept secrets of total success. In this book, I want to explode many of the major myths about attaining success and replace them with the basic truths that will guide you into living successfully no matter what your occupation, training, or abilities.

---

*H*appiness is the journey,
not the destination

--------------------- ✳ ---------------------

This book—*Being the Best*—is for everyone, from executives to middle managers ("one minute" and otherwise). It is for engineers, accountants, computer analysts, sales reps, clerks, and cab drivers, as well as people who serve our food or assemble our automobiles. It is for Aunt Martha, Uncle Charlie, and Cousin Jim.

And *Being the Best* is especially for mom, dad, and the kids (with apologies to the DINKS). This book could easily be tagged, "What we've always wanted our children to learn and remember, but we've sort of forgotten what it was."

We have forgotten because we too easily remember the ads and fads that undermine our real value, potential, and ability. The constant din of the myths stifles the truths. For example, the myth says:

YOU HAVE TO EARN YOUR VALUE BECAUSE YOU AREN'T
WORTH MUCH

but the truth is

YOU ARE BORN WITH INFINITE VALUE

and you only have to use what your Creator has given you.

We are far more likely to hear:

GO FOR THE JUGULAR—WINNING IS WHAT COUNTS

but the truth is

IF YOU GO FOR THE JUGULAR, YOU CUT YOUR OWN THROAT

and honesty and integrity are good old-fashioned values more precious than platinum.

Individuals often accept the crippling idea:

YOU'RE NOT GOOD ENOUGH; YOU'RE STUCK RIGHT WHERE YOU ARE

but the truth is

WHAT YOU SEE IS WHO YOU'LL BE

and you don't have to mindlessly buy into advertising carefully designed to convince you that since you are not among the beautiful, the swift, or the strong, you must try to rise above your mediocrity by using a certain product.

The myth makers smile when we say:

YOU CAN'T FIGHT CITY HALL; YOU'RE A VICTIM OF THE SYSTEM

but the truth is

YOU HAVE ALMOST LIMITLESS POTENTIAL

and you are never forced to do anything. You can choose your goals, lifestyle, job, and relationships.

Those content to live the myths parrot the shopworn cliché:

THANK GOD IT'S FRIDAY

but the truth is

THANK GOD IT'S TODAY

and every day is a new opportunity to reach your goals, make it happen, and find real purpose in life.

The myth can set the trap:

CHANGE IS FOR THE YOUNG, YOU'RE TOO OLD AND SET IN YOUR WAYS

but the truth is

YOU CAN REPLACE BAD HABITS WITH GOOD ONES

and with God's help, you can reshape your life with the right knowledge and positive attitudes.

Unfortunately, it's all too easy to be intimidated by the cynics who teach:

DO IT TO OTHERS BEFORE THEY DO IT TO YOU

but the truth is

DO IT FOR OTHERS AND THEY WILL COME THROUGH FOR YOU

because the golden rule applies in *every* sphere of life. No exceptions! We make a fetish of being cautious and tell each other:

TAKE CARE . . . DON'T STICK YOUR NECK OUT . . . DON'T RISK IT

but the truth is

FAILURE IS THE FERTILIZER OF SUCCESS

and you can take charge of your life by using your mistakes and disappointments to grow and succeed.

And, of course, there is always the old cliché so often used by coaches and trainers who ought to know better:

NICE GUYS ALWAYS FINISH LAST

but the truth is

NICE GUYS USUALLY FINISH BEST

because they use discipline, persevere, and make the most of their time to reach their goals.

THERE ARE MORE THAN TWO LEVELS IN LIFE

My goal in this book is to expose the myths that are enslaving us as a nation and as individuals and to reemphasize the ageless truths that can set us free. We can avoid the constant frustration caused by thinking there are *only* two levels in life—namely, *being on top* (#1, first, a winner and, therefore, a success) or *being inferior* (second best, runner-up, a loser and, ultimately, a failure) because one is on a rung below.

Even more important, we can be free from the deadweight of ambiguous personal standards—as we struggle to reach the top.

In her charming book, *Hope for the Flowers*,[3] Trina Paulus tells a parable that accurately exposes the futility of trying to claw your way to the top. When Stripe, the caterpillar, finds his normal routine dull and meaningless, he crawls off to discover the secret of life. He comes across other caterpillars who don't seem to know more about life than he does, but he joins a group of them who all seem to be crawling in the same direction.

Soon they come upon a towering column of squirming, wriggling caterpillars—a literal caterpillar pillar—that seems to rise forever into the clouds high above. The caterpillars seem to be desperately trying to crawl and wriggle over one another to reach the top of the pillar, and Stripe gets excited. Perhaps the top of the pillar is where he will find what he's looking for.

"What's at the top?" asks Stripe as another caterpillar wiggles by. Stripe's fellow crawler isn't sure, but "it must be awfully good because everybody's rushing to get up there."

Stripe hesitates a few moments and watches more crawlers pass him and disappear into the pillar. Finally, he decides there is only one thing he can do. He plunges into the wriggling mass of bodies to begin fighting his way up the column, being stepped on and stepping on others, as he climbs toward the top.

One day Stripe meets a friend called Yellow, and together they grow disenchanted with stepping on others, not to mention one another, as they fight their way to the top, whatever that is. They fall in love and decide to get out of the caterpillar race. Somehow they get back down to the bottom of the pile and go off to live happily—but only for a while.

Soon Stripe's boredom returns, and he wants to try the pillar again. Yellow tries to talk him out of it but to no avail. They part, and Stripe goes back to the wriggling, squirming caterpillar pillar to try his luck again to reach the top.

Yellow crawls off and discovers the secret of how to become a butterfly. While she spins her cocoon, Stripe fights his way back up the pillar. With ruthless discipline, he keeps stepping on others to reach the top. As he nears the very summit of the wriggling pinnacle, he realizes that he can't get to the absolute top unless he gets rid of those who are above him. Already he can hear the screams of falling bodies who have been displaced by the ones next in line. He is only a few wiggles from the top when he hears someone whisper, "There's nothing up here after all!"

Stripe stops wiggling and looks around. He is near the edge of the pillar, and as he gazes out beyond his own wiggling mass, he can't believe his eyes! All around him as far as he can see, the world is full of thousands of giant pillars just like his own, with countless caterpillars trying to reach the top.

Stripe doesn't know what else to do, so he turns back to work. Then he hears a commotion. He looks up and sees a beautiful yellow butterfly circling the pillar with effortless beats of its lovely wings. The butterfly comes closer and looks right into Stripe's eyes. Somehow those eyes are very familiar. Stripe isn't sure, but then something clicks inside. Could it be Yellow? Has she found the way to really live? There is only one way to find out.

Stripe turns and begins to fight his way back down the pillar. As he wriggles downward, Stripe tries to tell the others how futile it all is. He tries to tell them there's really nothing up there, but they are too intent on climbing. They think he's full of sour grapes. They know he just never made it to the top and he's jealous. Others aren't so sure. But they don't know what else to do. Even if it's true, they don't want to know that there is really nothing at the top. They *must* climb there because they don't know what else they can do.

And then one of the crawlers sneers at Stripe and tells him he's foolish to think he can be anything but a caterpillar. He's made to be a worm, and he should enjoy the caterpillar life.

Stripe wavers. After all, he has no proof he can become a butterfly. But he decides to continue fighting his way out of the caterpillar race.

Stripe eventually reaches the bottom of the pile, crawls off to find Yellow, and learns how to spin his own cocoon and emerge a lovely butterfly. The moral is quite clear. The "top" is not the lovely cradle of success that it's made out to be. There is really nothing up there, but to stay, you must watch out for usurpers, never relax, and become hard and cold because you're afraid that softness and warmth will be seen as weakness. Drop your guard for even a second, and those caterpillars below you will have you falling back to the rocks of failure below.

Trina Paulus's parable strikes such a chord because her simple story illustrates what I observe every week as I travel the country, talking to and with the people who are battling to be the best. To them, winning at any price is the *only* thing. And while all this going for the jugular, looking out for #1, and having it all continues unabated, we are losing something very precious. That "something" is the integrity, sensitivity, and camaraderie that built America into the greatest national experiment in inventiveness and industry in the history of this planet.

Success is not static, a particular level of achievement; the process is an ongoing one leading to wholeness. In fact, it has a variety of shapes, sizes, and colors.

THE BROWN COUNTY MARATHON

One of the best interpretations of success I have ever seen is a fourteen-minute sales training film that AT&T has allowed me to share in my seminars. The film recounts the running of the autumn marathon in a small town in Brown County, Somewhere, USA. Over one hundred runners are entered in the race, but in the film we focus on only three of them. There is a young woman whose goal for the day is to better her time by at least a few seconds. She knows that many of the marathoners can beat her former best time of three hours, fifty-three minutes. But she's hoping that today she can do at least 3:50 or 3:51.

---

*E*ach runner has a different finish line
—the goal each person has set

——————————— ✳ ———————————

Next we meet a young man who looks hopeful but not completely confident. His idea of success is simply finishing the marathon, something he has never done before. He isn't interested in running a 3:53 or even a 4:53. For him, success will be crossing that finish line and knowing that he has what it takes to complete the twenty-six grueling miles.

Our third runner is a young man who has come to "go for broke." He is not sure he can win, but he is intrigued by reaching down deep inside to see how good he really is.

The gun sounds, and all three runners break from the starting point with the dozens of others in the race. Soon they spread out along the highways of Brown County and settle in to run at their own pace.

Who wins the race? Not one of our three runners. A stranger, new to the area, crosses the line first. But does that mean all the others have lost? It depends on how you want to look at it. Externally, there can be one official winner who breaks the tape, but internally, the other runners know they win, too. The finish line that really matters is not the one drawn across the road back in town. Each runner has a different finish line—the goal each person has set. All three of the runners on whom we have focused have won, as well as the dozens of others who participated. The woman *did* better her best time by a few seconds; the man who just wanted to finish did; and the man who wanted to see how good he was pushed himself to a new level. For all three, the race was a process of achievement, of reaching an objective and creating the potential to move on to an ever-greater goal.

No runner is a loser. They all know the real prize in the race is not first place, but the race itself. They feel that special exhilaration, that refreshing high that comes from knowing they have done the very best they can do.

I BELIEVE THERE IS A WAY TO BE HAPPY

In the following chapters, I want to share essential truths and principles of a lifestyle that will help you run your own race at your own speed and win. I want to help you vault past the hollow self-help myths to the realities of being the best you can be. In these pages, I have tried to distill the essence of what I have been seeking to communicate for the past three decades.

In chapters 2 through 11, I want to share a forum, not just a formula, for being the best. Our round table discussion will include the following subjects:

- We must appreciate and believe in every individual's freedom and inner human worth.

- It is important to understand individual and collective responsibilities to one another.

- Victory is not gained only at someone's expense. Every victory does not result in a defeat. Being the best is identifying the talent or potential you were born with and using it as fully as possible toward a purpose that makes you feel worthwhile and at the same time benefits others.

- It is better to earn the trust and respect of one child than to gain notoriety and the adulation of the masses.

- Unless what you do serves as a healthy role model for your own children, it should not be done at all.

- In our status-oriented culture, beating others seems more important than being the best by sharing with and caring for others. We have become so addicted to immediate sensual gratification that we live in constant anxiety that can be relieved only by some successful accomplishment, adornment, or some kind of painkilling elixir.

- Success is not a matter of simply gaining financial wealth. (I know I already said that, but it's an idea that bears repeating.) I am not against money; in fact, I enjoy having enough of it. But money is like a train or plane ticket. It will take you nowhere unless you use it. A ticket does you no good if it is preserved and worshiped for its own sake. Money is also like a library card. Actually, money and knowledge are very much the same. They mean nothing when you simply collect them. They mean everything when you employ them, share them, and put them to work.

- Success is not the problem; it is what success does to us. Power and sharing are diametrically opposed. Sharing forces us to consider the needs of others, postponing or giving up some of our own desires.

- The former basis for defining being the best, according to external standards set by an ego-driven, highly impressionistic society, is being transformed.

- The new view of being the best is based upon God-given, timeless moral principles, which are consistent in that they take into account spiritual and ethical values affecting all humankind and the natural world.

I believe there is a way to be happy and contented. I believe we can master the skills, attitudes, and disciplines needed to be the best we can be. I believe there is a key that unlocks the door to all our dreams of satisfaction, happiness, and contentment. We can be whole persons who function more completely, effectively, purposefully, and gracefully. And when we can do that, we will understand success.

CHAPTER 2

*H*OW TO LIVE FROM THE *INSIDE OUT*_____

"HOW MUCH ARE you worth?"

Ask any group this pointed question, and you will get a variety of answers:

"None of your business!"

"Ask my tax man."

"Oh, maybe a few hundred thousand, I guess."

I attended a party once where one of the guests was worth $200 million—in cash. He taught me a lot about worth but very little about money.

An individual's worth has very little to do with salary, possessions, or position. Personal worth or esteem is something you have to recognize, appreciate, and enjoy, or your answer to the question, "How much are you worth?" will be, "Not much—probably nothing."

In recent years, particularly in America, a plethora of self-help books, tapes, and films have flooded the market, all designed to convince us that "God don't make no junk." In spite of all this positive input, the general public still believes the most damaging myth of all:

YOU HAVE TO EARN YOUR VALUE BECAUSE YOU AREN'T WORTH MUCH

What makes us believe this lie? We are born with all the value we will ever have, but life soon squeezes our feelings of self-worth and self-esteem like a juicer squeezes an orange. It starts as soon as we are old enough to hear our parents and teachers compare us to others: "Oh, isn't that little girl next door absolutely darling? I wish our Betsy had her nose." "Helen, don't bother me now. Can't you see Mother's busy?" "Harold, I'm surprised. Your brother was a whiz at fractions, and here you are flunking elementary math."

As we hit high school (in many cases it hits us), the erosion of self-esteem seems to pick up speed. I have made training videos with groups of high-school students and am almost always amazed at the lack of self-esteem they display. Some simply sit slumped in their chairs, staring at their hands folded in their laps. Others reveal how little they think of themselves and their fellow students by interrupting with rude and boisterous chatter and cute remarks. Or they may sit back with cool looks of disdain that actually hide a fragile self-image.

When I look back at my own youth, I remember how desperate we all were to belong to the "in group." Sometimes I clowned around and went to extremes to try to impress the most popular girls and boys in my class. When I was accepted, I felt great. When I was ignored and sometimes rejected, I was distraught. Today, with even more emphasis on material and physical appearances, young people are constantly vying for attention and recognition among their peers, as if there were a way to buy their way or "crash" their way into the elite winner's circle.

I'VE HAD MY OWN STRUGGLES WITH LEAKY SELF-ESTEEM

There is a vast difference, however, between wanting to be the best to bolster sagging self-esteem and seeking to live out inner worth and value by being the best we can be. We all have our struggles with this. I've had mine and still work at it. One reason I've spent much of my adult life studying human behavior and the difference between winners and losers is that I want answers to these questions for myself and my own life.

About ten years ago I began to develop the symptoms associated with an ego-driven individual. I wanted to be the best, and I made a conscious effort to impress others with my accomplishments and possessions. I became the center of my world, and I had to keep pumping up that center by blowing my own horn. Actually, I had leaky self-esteem.

People with high self-esteem have a high degree of modesty. They are not humble to a fault, but they do feel good about who they are and spend very little time talking about themselves or what they do. They don't have to. They spend most of their time listening to others, doing what I call paying value to others. They are good listeners. They are so busy making a quality contribution to life that they have little time for lining their den or office walls with trophies or press clippings.

But during this ego-driven time in my life (which lasted nearly two years), I started buying into the myths that say success means being rich, famous and #1. So I bought a big house and put a giant aquarium right in the living room window. I wanted everyone to know that I had an aquarium with saltwater tropical fish and that it took up an entire window of my house.

Of course I had an orange grove, hot tub, designer lawn furniture, a big swimming pool, and a shiny Mercedes. I could have parked the Mercedes in my garage, but instead I parked it out near the street so that everyone could see it. What good is a Mercedes in your garage where nobody can see it?

I also bought a horse and pastured it as close as I could to the road so people could drive by and admire our beautiful stallion. Or was it a gelding or a mare? I didn't even bother to look.

I got gates for our driveway—the big iron kind that people can't go through without pushing a button and asking for permission to enter. I thought that was the way to keep people impressed. I thought the laundry man would be impressed, so would the trash man, the United Parcel man, and any number of others I was convinced I should impress. Actually, I irritated them more than anything else, but I didn't know that at first. One day someone drove up, pushed the button, and ordered a Big Mac, a large order of fries, and a strawberry shake!

About the only one who could care less about my iron gates was the paperboy. He simply dropped the paper outside the gates and let me come clear down the driveway to get it. I ruined three pairs of slippers just getting my morning paper—ahhh, but they were Gucci slippers!

And so I had my castle and my own particular kind of "moat." Naturally, I decorated with lithographs of Picasso and other art objects designed to impress and turn heads.

When I was ready and I had my aquarium and my corral with a horse near the road and my Mercedes and coral in my bathroom that I picked up on my last trip to the South Seas and all the other trappings I thought meant success, I invited people over. I invited everyone I'd ever met, and some I hadn't, but that didn't matter much. The term *Yuppie* wasn't in use yet, but I was definitely a young, urban professional and I wanted everyone to know it.

My guests tramped in, dressed in their best. But I didn't understand that, often, they didn't come to see me and my wife Susan; they came to be seen and possibly gather some new tips on how *they* could look successful.

I spent the entire evening trying to impress them with what I had, where I'd been, and what I'd done. In two to three hours the crowd ate up $1,500 worth of hors d'oeuvres that I really couldn't afford, but I put them on my American Express Gold Card and was very impressed with myself. I didn't realize that the whole crowd had really come to get decorator ideas and to learn how they could make their own lives more impressive so that they could throw their own parties.

I went on like this for more than a year. The people I was trying to impress kept coming over and eating my hors d'oeuvres. When my saltwater tropical fish kept dying, I switched to the brightest and most colorful freshwater fish I could find because I still needed to have people see the aquarium that took up an entire window of my house. Actually, our cat was the only one who took real notice of the aquarium, much to the consternation of its occupants.

Then two things happened that helped me turn the corner on my journey toward success.

FASCINATING COUPLE . . . WHAT GREAT COMMUNICATORS!

The first incident involved having a couple over for dinner one night just after I'd returned home from a speaking trip. I was extremely tired, and instead of monopolizing the conversation and telling anecdote after anecdote, as I usually loved to do, I sat quietly and listened to the other people talk for a change.

As I listened, an amazing thing happened. I learned some new things about the couple. I learned that they were interesting, they had nice families, they were just as educated as I was, if not more so, and they had done things I had never done.

Susan and I listened for two or three hours, and I made only quiet comments: "Really?" or "My, that's interesting" or "Tell me more, give me an example."

They finally got up to leave, and as they went out the door and down the driveway, I ran to our master bedroom window to try to hear what they were saying about their evening. I was still somewhat insecure and didn't understand the difference between trying to impress and simply paying value to others. I wanted to hear what they had to say. After all, they might be talking about me!

I strained to listen, and as they opened their car doors, I could hear the husband tell his wife, "Weren't they the most fascinating couple you've ever met? What great communicators! Just delightful, marvelous people."

I looked at Susan, and she looked at me. I said, "But we didn't say anything except to ask questions."

And Susan said, "That's right. They went away feeling that we value them because we gave them our full attention all evening long."

I learned something that evening. I didn't tell one anecdote. I didn't share any chapters from any of my books. I didn't tell any Lee Trevino or John Madden stories. Nonetheless, those people went away saying, "Greatest people we've ever talked to."

After that night, I went back to doing more listening than talking. Listening to people had always been one of my strong points until I started reading my own press clippings. The trouble with reading your own press clippings is that you start to believe them and think that people are hanging on your every word. The truth is, most people want you to hang on *their* every word. And there is no better way to let them know that you are sincerely interested in them and that you care about them.

THE RICHEST GUY IN TOWN

The other incident that helped me stop trying to impress the world happened not long after the evening I just described. I was a guest in another home—a palatial estate owned by one of the richest men in our community. He wore more gold chains around his neck than Mr. T. He chewed on an extralong cigar that was never lighted. And he was big and tall and formidable—the perfect picture of what some success books call a powerful type.

Frankly, he had the biggest house I had ever seen. I was immediately depressed because the minute I went through his gates I started playing the game of "compare the status symbols." I could see that my place could fit comfortably in his wine cellar.

Another guest present that night was a farmer wearing a clean pair of jeans and a nice shirt, but hardly looking like someone who lived on

Rodeo Drive. What my host didn't know was that this farmer had owned all the land in the immediate area—one of the most expensive pieces of real estate in southern California. He had sold it all to developers and was worth over $200 million *in cash,* not holdings.

My host was doing the same thing that I had been doing, only on a bigger scale. He had invited all of us over to show us what he had attained. He wanted us to see the monument to his progress and success. To be fed the big barbecue dinner he had prepared, we all had to take "the tour."

Except for the farmer in the clean jeans, all of us were there not to pay our host value as much as to be seen and maybe pick up a few designer ideas. It was "Lifestyles of the Rich and Famous" without the cameras rolling, up close and personal.

The modestly dressed farmer joined us as we trooped through the house. He could have bought and sold everyone in the place, but you'd never know it. I asked around and people said, "He's the nicest guy in the world. You'd never know he had all that money."

I tagged along from room to room, trying to sort it all out. I was still a marginal being-the-bester who half believed that he who dies with the most toys wins.

Our host had a lot of toys. It took forty-five minutes to go through every room, including the master bedroom, the only bedroom in the house. Obviously, our host didn't want to have any guests. He did have twenty-five thousand square feet, a rotating bed, and skylights in the roof that opened and closed like automated draperies. The entire place was hermetically sealed and thermostatically controlled.

I was right behind the farmer, and I heard him mutter something about getting hungry. He had come to eat the barbecue and to see the special guests—a bunch of professional ballplayers shipped in for special impressive effects.

Our last stop meant going down the elevator into the wine cellar our host had created to look like one in a French chateau by flying in bricks, wood, barrels, and other building materials from a small village near Paris. We got out of the elevator, and I looked at more bottles of fine wine than I had ever seen in any Napa Valley winery. And I thought to myself, *Wow, what bucks! What success! What a winner!*

Then our host reached into one of the racks, which all rocked on cradles. (This storage method assures that sediment drifts to the bottom and thus maintains the crystal clear color of the wine.) He brought out a bottle and said, "This is a rare Pinot Noir reserve. It is perhaps the finest bottle of wine of its kind in the world. That's why it's worth $20,000."

The farmer had been standing there with the rest of us, and he said, "Let's go ahead and pop that one open. It must be pretty good stuff. You're a sly old fox. You were waiting to the end to bring out that $20,000 bottle of wine to toast your neighbors and friends. There are twenty-five of us here, and that ought to be . . . about $800 a glass. Let's do it. We'll each have a taste and toast in the new year and your good fortune."

Our host, with cheeks as pink as rosé, just looked at the farmer and retorted, "This isn't for drinking. It's for show. It's part of my collection."

The farmer looked him right back in the eye and said, "Well, I never invite people over to my house and show them my vittles unless I'm willing to share what I show them. I figure if you're going to show them some food or some drink, you ought to let them sample it."

Our host looked a bit chagrined and said, "Well, I'm sorry if I've misled you, but I just wanted to show you my collection."

The farmer sort of smiled and said, "Ah, shucks, and I thought you wanted to celebrate with us, not just impress us."

---

*T*he trouble with reading your own press clippings is that you start to believe them

---
✳

The farmer's words caused something to click deep inside me. We all took the elevator back up, but I left the party early. I went home and parked my Mercedes in the garage, put my stallion in the corral in the back lot, opened up the gates to my driveway, and took out my aquarium. It took me a while, but I finally figured out that the one with the most toys isn't a winner at all. Anyone who has a lot of toys, "just for show," and isn't really willing to share with others still has a lot of growing up to do.

SPAR WITH SUCCESS, DON'T EMBRACE IT

Back in the days of the aquarium and the Mercedes parked where everyone could see it, I thought I could be a success. Now I know that really isn't possible. I can have successful moments in certain arenas at certain times, but next week I may not fare as well. The market may go down. The investments can go sour. One of the kids could get hurt. The doctor could tell me, "Cut down on the calories and lose fifteen pounds."

To say, "I am a success," is to attach some kind of permanence to the word, as if nothing will ever change, as if things will always be the way they are now. But things don't stay the same. Everything changes— above all, success. When Robert Redford was named the top American motion picture box office drawing card, he told a TV interviewer that his ambition had always been to reach the top, and that to be the best he had to avoid being seduced by fame. Whenever he was tempted to believe his own publicity, he reminded himself that success is something he should spar with, but never embrace.

Success is fickle and fleeting, but living successfully by being the best you can be is always possible. To counter the myth that insists you must earn your worth, consider this simple but magnificent truth:

YOU ARE VALUABLE

Constantly remind yourself that you don't need gimmicks or possessions to build your self-esteem. You received all your worth and value when God gave you the gift of life. That gift—all of what's in you—is really all the value you will ever have. It isn't a matter of finding value, building value, or becoming valuable. It's a matter of living up to the value that was built in at the beginning. To do this is to be the best.

OKAY, I KNOW I'M VALUABLE, BUT . . .

Perhaps you are thinking that all this sounds good, but your self-esteem is still in need of some nurturing. Maybe it was all that bad input you got as a kid. Maybe the media have brainwashed you into a state of subtle cynicism or quiet desperation. Maybe you just lost a job, a love, or your reserved space in the company parking lot.

Then it's time to ask yourself some basic questions:

1. Am I valuable right now, just being me?
2. Am I capable—good at doing something well?
3. Am I respected by someone right now?
4. Am I loved right now—appreciated simply for who I am?

I believe that unless people have serious emotional problems, they can answer most or all of these questions in the affirmative to some degree most of the time. True, I may not feel the greatest about some (and possibly all) of these areas at a given moment. For example, I may not feel too capable, respected, or loved after my teenager has gone berserk with the car—again. Or an employer may not feel that her employees really respect her or think her very capable after the memo about the new overtime rules hits their desks.

What you and I must understand, believe, and act upon is that emotional reactions should not determine self-esteem. Spontaneous emotions are important, of course, but never confuse reactions with self-esteem, which is the constant, fixed value each person is given at birth.

As we were growing up, many of us played an inferior role to the adults in our lives. We were told what to do and what not to do. We were constantly reminded of our shortcomings. This emotional bombardment can take its toll, and if reinforced continually, can create the troubled teens, the generation gap, and stunted personal and professional growth.

Many people we know are hurt terribly by little things we call *social slights*. In my own research I have observed that the people who most easily become emotional and offended have the lowest self-esteem. People who feel undeserving—who doubt their own capabilities and have a poor opinion of themselves—become depressed, angry, or jealous with slight provocation. And jealousy, the scourge of every healthy relationship, is nearly always caused by self-doubt. People with inner value don't feel hostile toward others, aren't out to prove anything, can see the truth more clearly, and aren't demanding in their claims on other people.

Self-esteem is the gift you were given with all your value right at the start. It is knowing and believing you don't have a limit placed on you by somebody else. Your self-esteem is in your unique potential. It is in the clay itself, not the shape or design.

Some people think self-esteem belongs to those who have beautiful, successful, and talented parents. One of the greatest myths of all is that someone had it all going in. In other words, it was all on the surface; a background of good looks, rich family, and a lot of education and worldly wise knowledge was present at the very beginning. But that's not what I mean by the gift you were given up front. Your inner value has nothing to do with whether your mom or dad handed you a gold teething ring or an inexpensive pacifier.

The truth is, some people from the most unnurturing, humble beginnings have become the best human beings, and some people who have had the most fabulous starts have become the most pathetic failures. It all depends on what is done with God's priceless gift of inner value. Attitude and perception are critically important. Familial background, a "silver spoon childhood," Ivy League education, and so on are all secondary in the long run. Sooner or later each of us will develop a system of inner value, which reflects how we perceive ourselves and others. It is almost as though at any given time in our lives we can categorize just where we and others fit in the self-esteem arena.

If there were a scale or hierarchy of self-esteem, I believe it would resemble the chart I have developed to help illustrate undesirable and desirable value systems.

internalist altruist achiever	HIGH
materialist clown braggart	MARGINAL to LOW
cheat bully abuser terrorist assassin	LOWEST

Hierarchy of Self-Esteem

At the bottom level of esteem is the *assassin,* who is virtually devoid of feelings of inner value. The assassin wants to hurt others, especially important people, to gain self-importance.

Next comes the *terrorist,* who is just slightly higher on the esteem scale than the assassin. The terrorist needs to hurt or kidnap innocent victims to make a statement.

Up another notch is the *abuser,* who demands attention by mistreating people. Abusers slap people around, verbally and/or physically, to show power and to get their way. Through their violent behavior, they are trying to show how important they are.

Just above the abuser is the *bully,* who isn't quite as physical but who loves to intimidate. Bullies are usually cowards, but they come on strong to hide their fear and protect their fragile little portions of self-esteem.

Next is the *cheat,* who has to steal value from others to feel any importance. The cheat believes in "success at any price as long as it's free to me." The cheat is always on the "take" and never on the "give." Cheats never recognize their real worth or value. They try to get that value by stealing to gain success and achievement or money and property. Cheats are in all kinds of positions and situations, from marriages to stock brokerage firms, from tennis courts to probate courts, from wheeler-dealers to cat burglars.

In the middle level of the self-esteem hierarchy are people who don't need to kill, hurt, abuse, intimidate, or steal to get attention or gain feelings of self-esteem. They get it in more socially acceptable ways, but they can still be rather trying to live or work with.

First is the *braggart,* who boasts to get attention. The braggart loves to say, "Did you see what *I* accomplished, what *I* did, what *I* was wearing . . . ?"

Next on the scale is the *clown,* who is often a person others like to have around for entertainment. Clowns are often popular. What they're saying to the world is, "See me, I'm funny, please laugh." Clowns are usually well accepted by their peers—until they overdo it and cease to be amusing.

Up one notch on the scale is the *materialist,* who needs the superficial wrapping, the glitter, and the show to feel important. A lot of people fit in this category, though they may not admit it. I was in this category when I had my aquarium, my Mercedes parked where everyone could see it, and my big iron gates. I thought that to feel important, I had to impress people with my importance. How wrong I was!

On the high level of the self-esteem hierarchy is the *achiever,* who wants to be noticed for personal accomplishments. Achievers work hard to earn the respect of others. In fact, they are more interested in earning respect than they are in getting attention.

Achievers are often found on athletic teams or in sales organizations. Sometimes an achiever is regarded as one of the more underrated players on the team. Achievers may not get a lot of public or open recognition, but as long as they know their teammates and opponents recognize them as good performers, they are happy. While achievers don't really need to impress others, they do like recognition. They want some physical evidence, such as a trophy, a medal, a plaque, or a "well done!"

Even closer to the top of the self-esteem hierarchy is the *altruist*. Altruists don't need attention and recognition as much as they need the knowledge that others benefit from what they do. They are often very generous and self-giving, but their esteem depends to some degree on earning the approval and respect of others.

At the very top of the hierarchy is the *internalist*. (I'm not talking about an introvert or a young doctor just out of medical school.) Internalists know that the most important opinion always comes from within—from the conscience. Internalists are not cocky, conceited, or overbearing, nor are they unwilling to listen to the ideas of others. Their opinions of themselves, however, are based on internal standards rather than on what other people say about them.

Here is the summit of self-esteem. The internalist can say, "I gave it my best. I applied my full value and total effort to what I did. I have no regrets." This person's inner value system is secure and not subject to situations, changing moral climate, or societal pressures.

AN EMPTY BAG CAN'T STAND UP STRAIGHT

As you have considered the various levels of the self-esteem hierarchy, you may have been thinking, *I'm really not at the top right now. In fact, I think I'm somewhere down in the middle trying to impress, get attention, earn respect, or gain recognition.*

That's okay. If you can make an honest assessment of yourself, that's great! It gives you a starting point so that you can set some goals to rise higher on the self-esteem scale. You're not trying to rise above others so you can lord it over them. You're simply trying to become the best *you* can be, to accept and live out the full value given to you when you entered this world. Once you understand that, the more self-esteem you will have, and the more you will be able to give to others, which only builds your esteem even more.

Winston Churchill had a saying, "It's hard to expect an empty bag to stand up straight." If your bag is sagging a bit here and there, you have two choices: (1) you can hide—just avoid the issue and get by the best way you can, never really being able to lift your head up high and say, "I am valuable"; or (2) you can take inventory of your lifestyle and decide to do something about it.

SOME PRACTICAL DO'S AND DON'TS

Here are some practical tips to help you with your self-esteem:

Make enthusiasm your daily habit. The word *enthusiasm* comes from the Greek: *theos,* which means "God," and *entos,* which means "within." The capacity to become enthused is a spiritual quality generated from within; it doesn't need pep talks or perks. You sing because you're happy, and you also become happier as you sing. Enthusiasm, like smiling or laughing, is contagious.

I always seek genuine optimists as my friends. Homer Mitton, eighty-seven, who was my next-door neighbor some years ago, planted some orange and grapefruit seedlings in his backyard because he wanted freshly squeezed juice. No matter that it would be four years before the trees would bear fruit. He had the enthusiasm to believe he would still be around to enjoy them.

Well, I wasn't going to be outdone by an octogenarian. I dashed right out and bought a young redwood tree that I could also nurture to *full size.* And you know how long they live!

Don't let negative people determine your self-worth. Seek friends and associates whose lifestyles and words inspire you. If you have to deal with negative family members, fellow workers, or employers, make a conscious effort not to let them infect your thinking. See these people for who they are—lonely, unhappy, frustrated. Never tell yourself that you're "no good" because of treatment you have received from negative people.

T*he greatest communication skill
is paying value to others*

--------------------- ✳ ---------------------

Get into the habit of talking to yourself affirmatively. By talking to yourself, I mean the mental conversations you hold with yourself all day long. In recent years popular psychology jargon has called this self-talk. I like to call it scripting—writing your own script and playing out your own story to find a happy ending. (We'll be talking more about this later.)

Get into the habit of using an affirmative, positive vocabulary. Kids, employees, and associates don't need more critics and more negative input; they need better role models and more positive encouragement. I've included here some examples of words to stop using and words to use more often:

Words to Forget	Words to Remember
I can't	I can
I'll try	I will
I have to	I want to
should have	will do
if only	next time
problem	opportunity
difficult	challenging
stressed	motivated
I, me, my	you, your
hate	love[1]

Don't be a grudge collector. Too many people spend too much time every day thinking of past hurts, suffered-through office politics, messed-up relationships and, in general, the evils of the world. Don't waste your energy in this way. Apply your excellent mind to forgiving and forgetting.

Think positive and pleasing thoughts. Many people believe that Norman Vincent Peale was the originator of positive thinking. But Dr. Peale himself, a minister for some fifty years, would tell you that the apostle Paul was way ahead of him. In the first century, Paul wrote:

> Whatever things are true, whatever things are noble, whatever things are just, whatever things are pure, whatever things are lovely, whatever things are of good report, if there is any virtue and if there is anything praiseworthy—*meditate on these things.*[2]

Don't brag. Attention seekers need constant approval. Have the quiet confidence to let your actions speak for you. When you have real inner value, you don't need to flaunt an expensive imitation.

Get high on doing good. No one in history has found lasting satisfaction in chemicals or possessions. Real pleasure comes from good work, generous deeds, and grateful thoughts.

Don't give in to the ads and fads. Look for and listen for the truth. Rather than hear what you want to hear, listen for the facts of the matter. Everything you think is only your opinion, based upon your impressions from limited inputs. Always consider the source and credibility of your value system.

Wake up happy. Optimism is a learned attitude. (So is pessimism, so why not learn something that will help you?) Start thinking positively early in the day. If the alarm sets your nerves jangling, wake up to music instead. I strongly advise you to avoid listening to the morning news. It's almost always depressing. Listen instead to an all-music radio station or your favorite cassettes on your way to work.

Find a positive support group. Get involved with some positive peers who meet at least once a month for lunch or after work to discuss and brainstorm ways to achieve goals. Support groups that give me the most help include people from different ethnic groups, different lifestyles, different philosophies and viewpoints. At the same time I never share my problems with people who can't give me positive suggestions and direct me toward solutions. I always seek an optimistic, divergent, or different approach that inspires my creativity and imagination.

Above all, make every day and every evening the best possible. Once spent, they are gone. Once invested creatively, they bring a return much higher than any prime rate of interest ever will. Your attitude is either the lock on your door to high self-esteem and being the best you can be or the key that will open you up to more and more successful moments in life.

My optimistic neighbor, Homer Mitton, did live to have his fruit trees provide fresh squeezed juice to brighten his day. Always excited, with a smile on his face, Homer died while on the telephone with his travel agent, enthusiastically planning a trip around the world!

Homer would have agreed that your attitudes and perceptions can open up your life to all its possibilities. Instead of reaching for success, you will seek to live successfully. Don't waste time and energy reaching for the fantasies of a mythical success that cannot last. Determine to live from the inside out, moment by moment, being the best *you* can be!

HOW TO GIVE OTHERS POSITIVE REINFORCEMENT

Obstinate children, disruptive children, and slow-to-finish children may be brought into a spirit of cooperation with proper attention to positive expressions. Believe it when you say it:

- You outdid yourself today.
- You are improving every day.
- This a good paper, and it is neat.
- It looks as if you have been practicing because you are doing much better.
- I'm proud of the way you finished your work because I know you don't enjoy putting things away.
- This is complete. You haven't missed a thing.

Businesses, churches, and other groups need encouragement in a positive way, too. Say the following or post these comments on a bulletin board:

- You are working as if you are getting paid.
- That's the way to do it!
- I'm happy to see you working like that.
- You really make my job fun.
- That kind of (<u>work or behavior</u>) makes me happy.
- You did some first-class work today.
- We really did have a good day today.
- This must be one of the best departments we have.

Children who most often need praise seem to deserve praise the least. They tend to live out the low self-image they hold. Be careful; be positive; be without flattery in your praise. Call attention to the two or three things done right rather than the many things done wrong. Be an encourager with these words:

- The second time will be better.
- That's coming along well.
- You did several of them right.
- You are improving.
- I have never known anyone who tried harder.
- You have nearly mastered that.
- You are going to town—keep at it!

CHAPTER 3

CHARACTER CAN'T BE COUNTERFEITED

IN THE OPERATING room of a large, well-known hospital, a young nurse was completing her first day of full responsibility. "You've only removed 11 sponges, Doctor," she said to the surgeon. "We used 12."

"I removed them all," the doctor declared. "We'll close the incision now."

"No," the nurse objected. "We used 12 sponges."

"I'll take the responsibility," the surgeon said grimly. "Suture!"

"You can't do that!" blazed the nurse. "Think of the patient."

The surgeon smiled, lifted his foot, and showed the nurse the twelfth sponge. "You'll do," he said.[1]

* * *

A young woman, walking along the street of a large city, stopped a stranger to ask directions to a museum. The stranger said, "Go two blocks to the right and then turn left."

The woman continued on her way, but soon she heard the stranger calling to her. She turned around as the stranger caught up, panting for breath.

"I'm glad I caught you," he said. "After you started off, I realized that I had given you the wrong directions, and I didn't want you to get lost."[2]

* * *

A junior-high-school student had survived all the preliminary rounds of a national spelling bee, but in the final round, she misspelled a word. The judges, however, didn't hear her correctly, and they give her the nod. The contestant, realizing that she had misspelled the word, eliminated herself from the competition.[3]

✳ ✳ ✳

What do these three brief glimpses of life have in common? They all speak of a quality that is in short supply, and it's getting scarcer. But without this quality there is no way to be the best you can be. This rare quality is integrity—having a standard of personal morality and ethics that does not sell out to expediency and that is not relative to the situation.

As we closed chapter 2, we talked about the hierarchy of self-esteem, which has assassins and terrorists at the very bottom (zero self-esteem) and achievers, altruists, and internalists at the very top. When you reach the pinnacle of self-esteem, you have an inner standard for judging your performance. You are sure of what you can do, and the opinions of others do not hold you an emotional hostage.

Above all, you have a very precious commodity called self-respect. If you wanted to state your personal code of self-respect, it might sound like this:

MY PERSONAL CODE OF SELF-RESPECT
I am valuable because God created me with an inner value and worth. I do not have to earn it.

I nurture self-respect as I understand and internalize my basic inner value. The value is there. I don't have to achieve it. I already have it. My challenge is to nurture and protect it from getting jaded or twisted by the values of a success-at-any-cost-oriented society.

If I can avoid the trap of trying to possess success or adorn myself with success at the expense of others, I can easily live with self-respect. It will be more important to me to do things to project my value—the marvelous gift I've been given—to other people. That is the primary motivation for being the best I can be.

My worth is my word. I make commitments, and I do what I say I will do. This is more than just important to me—it is crucial.

I say to others: "I am valuable, as you are valuable. We will make a value exchange. I will offer you the best I have, and I assume you will give me your best in return."

People who see no or little value in themselves will not operate according to such a code. In fact, a code like this may be distasteful to them. Instead of being concerned with self-respect, they will try to gain recognition from others through manipulation, half-truth, and "show."

Unfortunately, a lot of people have their inner value system all mixed up, even inverted. For example, I find real confusion among the youths of our nation concerning self-respect. Teenagers' comments seem to indicate they believe that braggarts, clowns, and materialists are the winners in life.

They think that those who appear to be successful or popular have reason to be conceited. I often hear high-school students talking about someone who is good looking, popular, a real star, or "awesome." And in the same breath they say, "And do you know he actually *spoke* to me?" Do you see the conflict in this value system?

An absolutely critical developmental task of the adolescent is learning to see through the exterior and get to the heart of a situation or problem. Some young people learn to do this quite well and are not fooled by big talk, flashy or bizarre looks, distinctive clothes, and a pretty or a handsome face. Unfortunately, most do not. They move into adulthood thinking that the externals of life are what count. Isn't it interesting that the Bible says, "Man looks at the outward appearance, but the LORD looks at the heart"?[4]

HOW WE PANDER TO THE EXTERNAL

Anyone interested only in the external is doomed to live a shallow life. Men and women who lack genuine self-esteem and rely on their physical attributes to feel good about themselves inevitably will do everything they can to preserve their looks—the external—but will do very little to develop their inner value and worth.

This pandering to the external can be seen everywhere, and it is no more evident than in commercials on television and radio and in advertisements found in printed media. Beautiful models, actors, and actresses tell us in extremely subtle and clever ways that having a "certain look" is what counts. Of course, if we use a particular product, we will soon have all the admiration, sex, love—or whatever—we want.

Attractive role models gaze down at us from billboards and almost disdainfully dangle before our eyes the way to success. The answer is self-evident. We must buy designer label adornments to be one of the chosen few.

Can we count on these lovely images to deliver when the chips are down? We do not know. We cannot know because they are really figments of our imagination. Integrity is not the issue here; selling jeans or other products is. But integrity *is* the real issue.

Congressional witnesses huddle with their lawyers before facing inquisitors. Wall Street power brokers tremble in anticipation of another "insider trading" indictment. The Marines prepare to court martial one of their own for espionage. Christian ministries wince as the televangelist scandal occupies the national interest. And politicians, even front-runners for the nation's highest office, blatantly flaunt a dual moral standard while campaigning for American renewal.

What ever happened to basic decency, integrity, and an ethical conscience that clearly distinguishes right from wrong? According to a recent essay in *Time* magazine:

> Any moral crusade will run smack into the messages conveyed by America's celebrity-obsessed national culture. A few moments in the limelight can mean big bucks: a book contract, a speaking tour, a TV docudrama. All Fawn Hall had to do was reveal that she helped Col. Oliver North destroy documents related to the Iran-Contra affair, and suddenly Actress Farrah Fawcett was on the phone with plans to make Hall the heroine of a feature film.
>
> Sydney Biddle Barrows discovered there was even more money to be made from talking coyly around the subject of sex than in running an upmarket escort service. She sold her book for $250,000 and Candice Bergen portrays her in the film version of *Mayflower Madam*. Ethical distinctions are quickly lost as talk-show appearances and gala opening-night parties become schools for scandal.[5]

While the popular belief supports the myth that the only thing that counts is the bottom-line success, the truth is expediency leads to fleeting stardom and ultimate defeat. Integrity that strengthens an inner value system is the real bottom line in every arena.

A recent study of CEO's from many Fortune 500 companies indicated the most critical factor to consider in hiring or promoting top managers and in gauging the potential for their ultimate success is *integrity*. Ironically, traits that were ranked at the bottom in terms of importance were appearance, likability, and conformity. Interesting, isn't it, that the characteristics many adolescents, the general public, and the mass media emulate and find most attractive are the least likely to lead to genuine, enduring success.

THE YOUTH CRISIS: A REFLECTION OF ADULT VALUES

Nothing shouts louder about a nation's condition than the habits of its youths. And the habits of youths are nothing more than a direct reflection of the adult value system. The record needs no embellishing. We all know teenage pregnancy is an international epidemic, and the only proposed solution is the establishment of birth control clinics on high-school campuses.

To people of practical understanding, the relationship between price and demand is obvious. The notion that teenagers can be deterred from becoming pregnant by more and easier access to contraceptives and abortions is like expecting people who are given free gasoline to reduce their driving.

Every fifteen seconds a traffic accident involving an intoxicated driver takes place. Every twenty-three minutes one of our children dies in an automobile crash, and in most cases drugs or alcohol is involved.

Suicide is now the second leading cause of death among teenagers. And America is not alone in its youth crisis. The same is true in every other country in the so-called free world and behind much of the iron curtain.

These days, it is "snowing" all over the world as the number of cocaine users expands exponentially, with a marked increase in high school and even junior high school. After all, if "coke" is good enough for sports figures, show business stars, and the young upwardly mobile adults known as the beautiful people and the Yuppies, it's good enough for teenagers who desperately want to belong.

WHY DO SO MANY SELF-DESTRUCT?

What is causing this tidal wave of violent self-destruction and tragedy? The youth culture with its characteristic epidemics is merely a reflection of the new bankruptcy in morality and inner values. If there are no moral absolutes, if morality depends on the situation and circumstance, if people do what "feels good," ultimately they will lose their integrity and self-respect, and eventually this will lead to personal hopelessness and social chaos.

When self-respect is lacking, people have a long list of "wants."

They want love without commitment. They want benefits and perks without working for them; they want satisfaction without responsibility. They want to win the lottery with a one-dollar ticket. All they need is one winning hand. They want to feel good right away, and what could possibly feel better than the standing ovation given to a winner?

FAME VERSUS SELF-RESPECT

Fame has no necessary relationship to integrity, inner character, and self-respect. Examples are legion. From the rock music world, I think of Alice Cooper who disguises an average voice with a bizarre appearance, props, and special production effects. The "new" Alice Cooper show features Alice wrapped in a huge python, using illusions of witchcraft, the occult—anything that gets the imagination and powers of fantasy working overtime. And it seems to work. Newscasters probe Alice Cooper's psyche for what he's trying to do. "Entertainment Tonight" features him because he is "back." That's right, he's back with an even more obnoxious and revolting show.

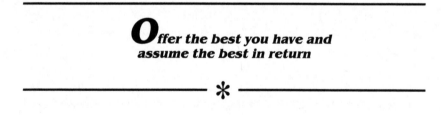

Offer the best you have and assume the best in return

The precious commodities of integrity and respect are often lacking in athletes. Tennis superstar John McEnroe, a brilliant player, is world famous for stamping and snorting and shouting obscenities calculated to intimidate. It doesn't matter whether he is angry with his opponent, the linesmen, or the umpire.

If anger is McEnroe's major weapon, outrageousness is quarterback Jim McMahon's. McMahon tries to get attention any way he can. He makes outrageous ads to sell motorcycles. He moons helicopters. He even criticizes his colleagues and supporters, yet his popularity seems undiminished.

For me, the price these famous performers pay for popularity and success is too heavy. They have swallowed the myth that says:

SUCCESS AT ANY PRICE; WHAT COUNTS IS RESULTS—THE SALE, THE BOX OFFICE, THE VICTORY

Like dry rot, this myth affects every facet of our society—business big and small, government, amateur athletics, professional sports. Even the church does not escape the win-at-any-cost mentality. Congregations vie for members and glory in their proselyting. And have you tested the integrity temperature in your local high school lately?

"WHY FAIL WHEN YOU CAN CHEAT?"

The win-at-any-cost myth leads many students to the notion it's okay to cheat to get ahead. Good students describe how they get the grades they need to go to a good college by using ingenious crib methods: putting answers on pencils, facial tissues, even calculator jackets. Stealing tests is standard procedure.

Do students cheat simply because they are corrupt, vicious, and no good? No, some of them cheat because they are too lazy to study. The majority of cheaters, however, justify it because of the pressure. There is pressure to get good grades in high school so they can go to a good college. There will be more pressure in college to get good grades so they can get a good job. And, of course, good jobs are hard to come by, and they certainly can't get any kind of job without that coveted college sheepskin.

Surely students don't cheat because they are stupid. They employ their native intelligence in countless ways to get on the honor roll or just to get by and get out. When teachers are lazy and do not change their tests year after year, students keep them and loan them or sell them to others.

Honor students candidly admit that there are few classes in which cheating isn't rampant. School policy may say that students caught cheating will automatically fail an exam and their parents will be contacted. Students continuing to cheat may be threatened with being withdrawn from an advanced class or barred from certain school activities. One wonders what students would do if they knew that cheating meant automatic final expulsion from school, no chance to ever earn any kind of degree?

Most school administrators, however, don't want to make those kinds of waves. They prefer to go on, brandishing their rule books, but seldom enforcing the rules. The result? Everyone keeps selling out integrity on the cold, hard altar of expediency. One student said it all when he shrugged: "I don't understand why people fail when they have the opportunity to cheat."[6]

It's time to issue a warning call:

SUCCESS ALWAYS HAS A PRICE; WHAT COUNTS IS INTEGRITY

With success at any price as the goal, there is no room for integrity. Without integrity, there's no place for self-respect. Without self-respect, there can be no valid self-esteem. The result? Moral and spiritual bankruptcy. Being the best you can be is a hollow fantasy.

But we can turn the tide for integrity. We have to look for, listen for, and bring to the attention of those who respect our opinions case histories in every walk of life illustrating integrity in action.

Some time ago, a *National Racquetball Magazine* article told the story of Reuben Gonzales who was in the finals match of a professional racquetball tournament. It was Gonzales's first shot at a victory on the pro circuit, and he was playing the perennial champion. In the fifth and final game, at match point, Gonzales made a super "kill" shot into the front wall to win it all. The referee called it good. One of the two linesmen affirmed that the shot was in. But Gonzales, after a moment's hesitation, turned around, shook his opponent's hand, and declared that his shot had "skipped" into the wall, hitting the court floor first. As a result, he lost the match. He walked off the court. Everybody was stunned.

The next issue of *National Racquetball Magazine* displayed Reuben Gonzales on its front cover. The editorial searched for an explanation of this first-ever occurrence on the professional racquetball circuit. Who could ever imagine it in any sport or endeavor? A player, with everything officially in his favor, with victory in his hand, disqualified himself at match point and lost!

When asked why he did it, Reuben said, "It was the only thing I could do to maintain my integrity."

In my opinion, Reuben Gonzales may have lost that match, but he won something far more important. He maintained his self-respect, and he also gained the respect of his peers, his sport, and those in the general public fortunate enough to have watched his example as a role model.

INTEGRITY BEGINS AT HOME

What can we do to increase the dwindling amount of integrity in the world today? Like charity, integrity begins at home. One of the greatest gifts we can give our children is strong moral and ethical values. Let them accept responsibility for their own actions as early as possible. The more responsibility they develop, the better they will feel about themselves.

Accepting responsibility begins early as the toddler learns to do basic chores, such as picking up and putting away toys. It's learning to put dirty clothes in the hamper and maintaining a sense of orderliness. As children grow older, they can perform regular chores and learn how to handle money. Never do anything on a regular basis for your children that they are capable of doing for themselves. Your role is to help them become independent, self-sufficient adults who can share their values with others out of mutual respect, not out of dependency.

Above all, for integrity's sake, teach them graciousness and gratitude and how to share and care about the rights and welfare of others. Teach your children that their true rewards in life will depend on the quality and the amount of service they render and that they should always treat others as they would have others treat them. Every "right" has its equal responsibility.

Tragically, many parents raise children with a special-interest-group mentality. Children learn to be more concerned with their rights than their responsibilities. Rights without equal responsibilities are euphemistically called entitlements. Motivated by fear, laziness, and greed, more and more people are coming to accept poor productivity, shoddy workmanship, and low or no moral values as standard. Integrity is being replaced by the something-for-nothing, if-it-feels-good-I'll-do-it myths running rampant in the Western world.

THOU SHALT SET A BETTER EXAMPLE

If I were writing "Ten Commandments for Parents," one of the most important would be this: thou shalt conduct thyself in such a manner as to set an example worthy of imitation by thy children. In simpler terms, if your kids shouldn't be doing it, neither should you.

When I told my kids to clean their rooms, for example, they took a closer look at the state of disarray in the garage.

When I told them that honesty was our family's greatest virtue, they commented on the radar detector I had installed in my car, and they took a real interest in the way I filled out my tax returns.

When I told them not to engage in taking drugs and drinking, they watched from the upstairs balcony the way our guests behaved at our adult parties. I think they even checked the medicine cabinets to see what medications we took, both prescription and nonprescription.

It didn't matter how young they were. My kids were processing my input to them before they could even walk or talk. In my lectures and the "Psychology of Winning" audiotapes, I relate the true story of the role-model confrontation I had with one of my daughters, Dayna, when she was still in her high chair.

I'll never forget that fateful day. First, I should prepare you for the situation comedy that developed between me and my nine-month-old child. I was a hot-shot naval aviator who thought he commanded the skies and his family. I wore my flight suit to mow the lawn to impress the neighbors. I sometimes wore my flight helmet, with a bolt of lightning painted on each side, while driving my black Porsche, and I went out of my way to intimidate Volkswagens on the freeways.

It was early Friday evening, and I had just arrived home from another jet-jockey day of chasing farmers on their tractors (pretending they were Soviet SAM missile launchers) and doing what we did to make our nation more secure.

Pulling into the driveway, I immediately headed for the kitchen. With all that "combat" flying, I had generated a ferocious appetite. Well, you can imagine my stunned reaction when I saw my wife sitting patiently in front of our daughter's high chair with strained squash in her hair, all over the front of her apron, on the floor, and not one spoonful in our daughter's mouth. Dayna was holding her mother hostage, threatening more "squash-fire" unless the applesauce and Oreo cookies were delivered immediately.

As a not-yet-reformed, semichauvinist navy pilot, I grabbed the spoon out of my wife's hand to show our baby mutineer who was in command. "Open up. It's your dad," I ordered sternly. Her gums clamped shut in defiance. My wife smiled sweetly and kept score.

I shifted from intimidation to inspiration as a positive role model. I tried success-by-association techniques. As I ate half the jar of squash, I made chortling, lip-smacking noises of approval. (Actually, I nearly gagged. The stuff was gooey and bland.) As I demonstrated how delicious strained squash tastes, I searched her face for any hint of acceptance that would surely follow. Instead, I got the "Okay, fatso, if you like it . . . *you* finish it" look!

That did it. I put on my flight helmet and told my wife to leave the kitchen. It was a restricted war zone now!

I squared off against my nine-month-old. Pushing her cheeks together firmly with two fingers, I gently but firmly forced her mouth open. I quickly inserted three heaping spoonfuls of squash and then held her mouth shut, like many fathers and mothers before me had done to their children.

Her response was immediate and uncompromising. She decided to hold her breath indefinitely and risk brain damage rather than swallow. Her face began to turn red and purple. My face also turned red and purple with exasperation. I glared at her, nose to nose, eyeball to eyeball.

"It won't do you any good to hold your breath, sweet child. You have to breathe sooner or later, and besides, you're not the only child, you know!" Talk about a parent out of sorts and out of control. I actually said those words, out loud.

And may the Lord smite me down if she didn't understand and act accordingly. She exhaled suddenly, just as I exerted more pressure on her cheeks to keep the squash in. Are you familiar with linear acceleration? When you squeeze a propellant so that the orifice through which it travels is very small and the pressure is great, you get the nozzle effect.

All I remember is that as she exhaled, a steady stream of strained squash fired up both my nostrils and continued into my nasal passages headed for my pituitary gland. I fell to the floor choking and gasping for breath. My wife had tiptoed back into the kitchen to watch the show and looked down at me lying prostrate and bellowing like a wounded bull.

"What happened, Top Gun?" she teased.

"Nothing happened," I replied weakly, regaining the use of my nose and my composure as I reached for a tissue. "Don't make a big deal about it. She doesn't like strained squash."

I learned a great lesson from that ridiculous incident. First, children reflect the behavior present in their environment. Second, they do have minds of their own. They can accept or reject our teaching. That's why it is so important to set a good example by our actions every day.

Easier preached than practiced. We go along for a while setting a good example, but sooner or later we start telling ourselves we need a break. We need to let down our hair—go out and be ourselves for a change.

The trouble is, the kids get confused. They think mom and dad are being themselves by modeling good behavior. When they see the other kind, they are puzzled at first, but then they catch on. They learn to play the game of "say one thing, do another."

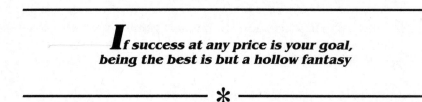

If success at any price is your goal, being the best is but a hollow fantasy

The old cliché says it all: what you are speaks so loudly no one can really hear what you say. But it is even more true that if what you are matches what you say, your life will speak loudly indeed. You can use the following tips to teach your kids by word and action.

Teach your children to do their best in everything. Then be sure to do your best.

Never say, "As soon as you get your work done, you can go out and play." *Say, "There is a time for work and a time for play. We give our best to both every day."* Then don't neglect to cut the lawn or wash the windows because you want to watch the ball game on television.

Teach that there are no shortcuts to success. Being successful requires knowledge, preparation, and persistence. (If you're really serious about this one, don't bank on the lottery.)

Limit the family's TV viewing to special shows. Never allow family members to use TV as an escape mechanism to get away from important and enriching projects.

Teach your family the simple truth that winners work hard to be successful.

Whatever you do, do only what can be observed by your children to their benefit. Then when you have to say "I think this is what you should or shouldn't do for your own good," they are more likely to believe you.

"BUT, DAD, ALL THE KIDS ARE GOING TO THIS PARTY!"

Some time ago one of our teenage daughters became upset because I wouldn't allow her to attend a party at a girl friend's home after I learned that the parents would not be present.

"We're not little kids," she pouted. "We know how to be responsible. Why can't I go? Don't you trust me?"

"I trust you, but I don't trust the situation," I said carefully. "Your mom and I believe we should be on the premises and available when you give parties here for your friends. Frankly, I am not sure I trust parents who would let their child give a party when they're not there.

"Let's suppose your mother and I left while you gave a party. What if someone started fooling around and got in trouble in the pool? What if someone got hurt? We would feel guilty for the rest of our lives. We're responsible for everything that goes on in our home. We don't want to abdicate that responsibility and give it to you at your age. We know you're a responsible person, but we don't think it's fair to put you in a position of taking responsibilities that are really ours."

"But I'm not the one who is responsible—Brenda is," our daughter responded.

"No, I don't agree. Brenda's *parents* are really responsible, and if they're not going to be there, they are putting her in a position that we would never require of you. We wish they would consider doing what your mother and I do when you have a party. They could spend the evening in another part of the house but be available for any emergencies or help with food and such."

Somewhat reluctantly, our daughter bought our logic. She wound up staying home from that party, and Susan and I felt relief, not guilt.

Teaching your kids integrity is not easy, but it's worth every effort because there is no better way to build their self-esteem than to help them build self-respect. Of course, it doesn't hurt *your* self-respect either. As I try to pass on integrity to my children, I keep this idea in mind: what I leave *in* them is more important than what I leave *to* them.

Rate yourself on the ten-question test of personal ethics developed by William D. Brown, a clinical psychologist. It is interesting to analyze this test in the light of how it reveals one's self-esteem.

When it comes to being tempted to pad an expense account, each person is guided by conscience. Some people have more highly developed consciences than others. It is fairly safe to assume that if you are interested at all in your level of integrity, your conscience is quite tender. To violate your conscience is to lower your feelings of self-esteem.

If you are concerned about integrity and being the best you can be, a full day's work for a full day's pay is standard procedure. Performing at less than anything but your highest level is bound to result in damage to your feelings of self-esteem.

Dwight L. Moody, the Billy Graham of the nineteenth century, once said, "Character shows—even in the dark." Pilfering even the smallest items is no way to build self-respect or self-esteem.

You probably marked question 4 with a 5 (strongly agree) because you are quite sure you would never actually misappropriate even the

---

TEST YOUR INTEGRITY LEVEL

Fill in each blank with a 5, 4, 3, 2, or 1, using the following scale: 5 = strongly agree; 4 = agree; 3 = uncertain; 2 = disagree; 1 = strongly disagree.

1. I don't give in to the temptation to pad my expense accounts. ____
2. I do a full day's work for a full day's pay. ____
3. I never take office items—even small ones—for personal or family use. ____
4. If my fellow workers were as honest as I, our company would never have to worry about white-collar crime. ____
5. Those who know me consider my word my bond. ____
6. "Loyal and faithful friend" is one way my friends would describe me. ____
7. Recognizing how readily we influence the behavior of others, I strive to set a good example in all my endeavors. ____
8. Each day, I work at remaining honest in all interactions, both in and out of the office. ____
9. If my spouse's emotional and physical fidelity were equal to mine, I would be satisfied. ____
10. In general, my approach toward others—both at home and away from home—is to treat them the way I would like to be treated. ____

TOTAL ____

You should score this test as follows:
    44–50—*Excellent.* You are undoubtedly a winner.
    37–43—*Good.* But there's room for improvement.
    0–36—*Poor.* Your integrity is sadly lacking.

smallest amount of money. But consider the question again and ask yourself: Am I really more honest than my fellow workers? What if I had a real emergency and no one would ever know if I took a few dollars?

One of the highest compliments you could ever be paid is to be told that you are a person of your word. Too many people say that they will do something, but later they give excuses like these: "Oh, I didn't realize you really meant that" or "That isn't exactly what I had in mind." Talk is cheap, but going back on your word is expensive because it costs you your self-respect.

A true friend has the ability to keep a secret and is someone who can be counted on—in good and bad times.

Deeds are always more important than words. And deeds reveal how much you really value yourself.

There is no better way to set an example for others than to be honest. Honesty doesn't just happen; it is often displayed at tremendous cost and with real sacrifice. Every time you do the right thing instead of the wrong thing, you strengthen everyone and pay tribute to your inner value and self-esteem.

Fidelity in marriage may be growing more scarce than integrity in professional life. Affairs and adultery are riddling families in epidemic proportions. If you are truly concerned about fidelity to your spouse, observe one important rule: Never let friendships with others supersede your relationship with your spouse. Make your spouse your best and most trusted friend; best friends do not stab each other in the back.

The double standard of having professional and personal lifestyles that don't match is irrevocably dead forever. Integrity is not an option. Integrity is not situational. Integrity is an absolute standard for those who really understand what being the best is all about.

Several decades ago, Madame Chiang Kai-Shek, who along with her husband led the Chinese people in their struggle against the invading Japanese army during World War II, put integrity in a golden nutshell when she said,

> In the end, we are all the sum total of our actions. Character can't be counterfeited, nor can it be put on and cast off as if it were a garment to meet the whim of the moment. Like the markings on wood which are ingrained in the very heart of the tree, character requires time and nurturing for growth and development.
>
> Thus also, day by day, we write our own destiny; for inexorably . . . we become what we do.[7]

*

LISTEN TO THE CHILDREN

Take a moment to listen today
To what your children are trying to say

Listen today, whatever you do
Or they won't be there to listen to you

Listen to their problems, listen for their needs
Praise their smallest triumphs, praise their smallest deeds
Tolerate their chatter, amplify their laughter
Find out what's the matter, find out what they're after

But tell them that you love them, every single night
And though you scold them, make sure you hold them,
And tell them "Everything's all right."

If we tell our children, all the bad in them we see
They'll grow up exactly how we hoped they'd never be
But if we tell our children, we're so proud to wear their name
They'll grow up believing they're winners in the game.

Take a moment to listen today
To what your children are trying to say
Listen today, whatever you do
And they will come back to listen to you!

CHAPTER 4

Living WITHOUT LIMITATIONS

ONE OF THE few times I watch television is while I'm shaving and getting dressed in my hotel room before presenting a morning seminar. On one particular day, I was to teach a three-hour session on the effects of negative media bombardment and cynicism on the self-image of youths and society in general. While my Remington clipped my whiskers "close as a blade, or my money back," I was taking in the nationally syndicated network talk shows to catch a glimpse of what was generating those fabulous ratings in morning prime time.

What a lineup on our male hero's program! How fortunate for the studio audience to be able to be there live to interact and benefit first-hand! What a break for me to have tuned in by sheer chance! I could research what the American population really is thinking about!

The first segment of the show featured four part-time prostitutes. In the evenings and on the weekends, they were upwardly mobile suburban housewives. But during the weekdays they were turning tricks as urban call girls. Our roving silver-haired interviewer orchestrated the exchange between the distinguished panel of experts and the studio audience. "Should the part-time housewives-hookers tell their husbands about their professional hobbies?" "Should they put their earnings in their joint checking accounts?" "Were they bored or just trying to get even with their workaholic spouses?" "Did any of their children suspect that they weren't just off to the food market?"

I was about to turn off the set and go for a walk when the guests for the second segment were announced to the cheers, whistles, and stomping feet of the normally dignified live audience. Five male strippers were cavorting around in theme G-strings. The rationale, of course, was what's good enough for the gander is good enough for the goose to gander at. Not in the mood for this kind of cultural overload, I switched channels to see what another network's talk show host had to offer.

There they were seated on the stage, each one a big winner and new millionaire via the state lottery. She brought them all together for one of her season-opening shows so America could get inspired to face a new year by hearing their success stories.

"How has this changed your life?" "How are you going to handle all this success?" "What are you going to buy first?" "What advice can you give to the rest of us if we win the jackpot?" The host was playing it straight and asking all the right questions.

And while the happy winners shared plans to buy new homes or cars and to take trips to Aruba, eager viewers across the land joined the studio audience on the edge of their collective seats, straining to catch every word of these secrets of success. This was something we could all look forward to—if we were lucky enough. We, too, had a chance to get rich and savor true success.

I'm certain that both programs got good ratings, but what did they really accomplish? The insights into lifestyles of part-time prostitutes and male strippers did little to promote viewer self-esteem or self-respect. And the parade of those one-in-a-million lottery winners once again programmed the viewer to believe the myth that trumpets:

ONLY THE LUCKY OR TALENTED FEW CAN BE SUCCESSFUL

This myth tells us success means getting rich quick, signing the contract for $1.8 million a year for twelve years. Success means having your ship come in, being lucky, being in the right place at the right time. This myth teaches us that if we want to experience success, it must be doled out to us in the form of talk show guests and thirty-to-sixty-minute sitcoms and soap operas. Denigrated, ignored, and neglected is the real truth about the vast human potential God has given to all of us:

SUCCESS IS WORKING HARDER OR SMARTER—USUALLY BOTH—AT WHAT YOU ENJOY AND ARE GOOD AT

I see and hear of examples of this truth every day. Not many receive media coverage, but I get excited and inspired learning about so-called common people who are so uncommon in pursuit of being their best. And it doesn't matter how lucky or talented they are.

Barbara Schein, a grandmother, aged fifty, made it through four and one-half months of physical training to become the first woman of her age to fulfill all requirements as a police officer in the state of New Jersey. She had always wanted to do police work, but "they didn't take many women" when she was younger. So she settled for being a homemaker, rearing two daughters, and selling insurance part-time.

Later she inquired again about a police career but found she was over the state's age limit of thirty-five. For the next twelve years, she did part-time work as a special officer directing traffic and helping maintain order at basketball games. When the age limit was labeled discriminatory and dropped, Mrs. Schein passed a written test and tried for an opening with the North Haledon (New Jersey) Police Force.

At five feet tall she was trim from daily exercise, but the police academy was grueling. After running up to five miles a day and performing calisthenics, she came home exhausted and irritable. Her husband, Edward, supported her efforts throughout the ordeal, even though "he never thought it would end."

She graduated with ninety-one others, almost all of whom gave her full support and approval as a fellow officer. Her chief says most of the fifteen officers she works with today have accepted her, and he believes she can "handle her own."[1]

Barbara Schein does not fit the media stereotype of who or what she ought to be. Because she felt good about her personal potential, was confident that she could accomplish her goal, and worked hard to reach that goal, she succeeded.

TV commercials are carefully designed and expensively produced to help us "realize" we are far less than we should be. Our potential is not within ourselves. Our potential is rated by how many new potions, lotions, or notions we buy. TV viewers have potential, all right—as a potential market.

When I criticize the greater percentage of TV programming available today, I am not suggesting that we sell our television sets to gain a better sense of self-worth. But I am suggesting that we become more selective in what we watch and more discerning as to what programs and broadcasts are doing to our self-image and sense of potential. In fact, a good way to test any program is to consider these ideas:

Am I being uplifted, inspired, or challenged to live up to my internal value, gain and maintain self-respect by having more integrity, and realize my potential to be the best I can be?
OR
Am I being subtly told that I have real little inner value, that I must prove my worth in a dog-eat-dog world, that integrity is for nice guys willing to finish last, and that I have potential only as a spectator who can wait for a lottery ticket to have the winning number?

There are no more powerful purveyors of stifling and limiting inputs than the media, as ironic as that may sound. Trumpeting the public's right to know, reporters and hosts of all kinds use television, radio, and the press to keep the exposés coming almost faster than we can take them in.

Many members of the media appear to feel they can't enhance their careers and their ratings until they can uncover and scoop the competition with a juicy scandal to capture the eyes, ears, and emotions of the general public. Forget about the positive track records and accomplishments; go for the jugular by focusing energy on discrediting the powerful.

In a free society, corruption must be uncovered before it takes root, and the rights of innocent victims must be protected. But the pendulum has swung far past any acceptable limit. News making has gotten out of hand and turned into ratings making. The occasional warm, human interest piece is overwhelmingly outnumbered by reports of carnage, catastrophe, tragedy, and intrigue.

This negative bombardment of the senses not only creates uneasiness, guilt, and depression among impressionable members of society, but it also generates a morbid malaise throughout the nation. It is like acid rain or Agent Orange falling on our heads and permeating our minds.

I am also convinced that commercial programming shows society examples of being the worst rather than offers any selection of role models to help us in being the best we can be. Some of the programs are good, but most of them are bad. As you watch for education, entertainment, or escape, ask yourself: Does this program portray reality as I know it? As my family and friends know it? Or is this somebody else's idea of reality that I am being asked to accept as the norm? Am I getting the kind of television programming I really want? Or am I getting what a relatively small number of writers, directors, and producers call real life?

WE ARE GETTING WHAT A FEW CALL REAL LIFE

I am firmly convinced that the few who control the media are telling the many who watch, listen, or read: "We are simply reflecting your society as it really is. This is what you are really like, this is who you really are, and this is what you are willing to pay for."

TV commercials are carefully designed and expensively produced to help us "realize" we are far less than we should be

——————— ✳ ———————

It is high time to challenge the assumptions, precepts, and value systems of those who produce TV programming and other media. Don't just automatically swallow what they give you and think, *Wow, so that's how it is today. People are* really *sick.* Some people *are* really sick, but the challenge is to identify which ones. Ask yourself why so many television programs and films present degrading lifestyles, indulgence, drugs, and permissiveness in such a positive, attractive, sympathetic, or exciting light. Does this programming show life as it really is, or does it reflect the value systems, imaginations and, in some cases, the personal struggles of the people producing them?

Television producers, filmmakers, recording stars, and slick magazine publishers go unchecked and unchallenged in telling us, "It's a concrete jungle out there. Unless you are one of the beautiful people, you have no future or real potential." They add, "You have no permanent value. You are limited by background, parents, looks, and IQ. You need to get the breaks, have it happen, get lucky." They perpetrate this giant myth:

YOU HAVE CERTAIN LIMITATIONS YOU CANNOT OVERCOME

The truth, however, is much different. For one thing, being one of the beautiful people gives you no guarantees of success or even peace and contentment. Many of the so-called beautiful people are the most messed-up individuals on the face of the earth.

The truth is, you have built-in inner value, and because of that value, you can enjoy self-respect. You have tremendous inner worth, and if you are living up to that inner worth with integrity, which leads to self-respect, your potential is practically limitless. Canceling out the giant myth is an even greater truth:

YOU CAN LIVE FAR BEYOND ANY SO-CALLED LIMITATIONS

I am not saying there are no limits at all. All of us face certain limits. I will never become a star in the NBA or run a hundred meters in nine seconds or pole-vault twenty feet. But I have done many things and I can do many more. I am just starting to uncover my real potential.

THE DIFFERENCE BETWEEN LIMITS AND LIMITATIONS

Even my no-limits colleague Wayne Dyer admits that you should not do or be something for which you are not gifted or suited. Wayne doesn't suggest jumping off cliffs without hang gliders or walking on water without skis. His best-selling book is entitled *The Sky's the Limit*, but he is talking about developing your God-given value and potential as fully as possible—becoming the best you can be. He believes—and I agree—that you should let yourself arrive fully into life instead of just hanging around the edges thinking you aren't quite good enough to compete in the big leagues. You should give yourself permission to reach the highest levels you can conceive and attain.

Perhaps it helps to see there is a difference between limits and limitations. You cannot surpass certain *limits* because you simply are not physically or mentally equipped to do so, but that doesn't mean you have to squander and stifle your real potential by living according to certain *limitations* inspired by yourself and others. You can learn to live without limitations. *Limits* are physical boundaries, such as high-jumping ten feet. *Limitations* are psychological impediments, such as feeling unworthy of material or emotional success.

If you are to overcome the externally imposed limitations the world lays upon you, you must not play the comparison game of matching your potential and self-image against those of the two categories of impostors on television. At one extreme are the beautiful and all-powerful who seem to have no human limits. At the other end of the continuum are the fouled up, the incompetent, the criminals, and the losers.

Compare yourself favorably with the losing extreme, and you risk becoming arrogant and uncaring. Compare yourself unfavorably with the superwinners, and you risk depression or frustration by continually looking at your "deficiencies."

To be the best at developing your potential, consciously avoid judging yourself against the fantasies presented on the television screen. They are exaggerations of the lives of the superbeautiful, superrich, superstrong, and superpowerful that can't be realized by even 1 percent of the population. Even if you could attain superhuman levels, you wouldn't enjoy them because you would feel lonely and superficial. Real people simply don't live like that.

Reality says you have the potential to become infinitely more than you are now. Animals are programmed by instinct, but human beings can develop God-given abilities through observation, imitation, and reasoning. The greatest limitations you will ever face will be those you place on yourself. Only you can stifle your potential. Remember, it takes just as much time and effort to lead an average or mediocre life as it does a good one.

When I talk about my potential, I am forced to be specific. I must relate my self-esteem and self-respect to very tangible and measurable images I have of myself. How do I match my sense of self-worth with the realities of my life—the external and material that ask me how much money I make, what kind of job I have, how attractive I am? What are my physical and mental strengths? How does my personality affect others? It helps me to make a sharp distinction between my self-esteem and my self-image, two terms that are often used interchangeably. My *self-esteem* is my inner value, worth, and potential; my *self-image* is how I see myself succeeding or failing at the tasks and challenges of life.

Actually, I do not have a single self-image. It is probably more correct to say I have several self-images. I see myself as a good singer or a monotone. I see myself as able to draw well or like a first grader. I have a self-image about my ability to speak, write, fix the car, or make love. My self-images say, "Yes, you do that quite well, perhaps very well," or "No, you are only so-so or very poor in this other area."

The three big questions you must ask yourself regarding your potential are (1) who am I?; (2) what am I?; and (3) why am I? To answer all three, you must go to the heart of your spirit and your potential. What you imagine, internalize, and put into practice is what you will eventually realize and experience for yourself.

This can work for you or against you. The mind has an amazing quality: it doesn't automatically gravitate toward truth, right, justice—the best. It gravitates toward what it is exposed to the most. The development or nondevelopment of your potential is linked directly to what you allow yourself to be exposed to.

WHAT IS HAMPERING YOUR STAR TREK?

I once appeared on a program with a group of teenagers to discuss career choice and discovery. I asked them, "What is holding you back or impeding you in your quest for success? What is hampering your star trek?" Their answers centered on the following: fear of nuclear war; economic problems, such as the deficit, inflation, high interest rates; violence and crime; drug abuse; pollution—the proliferation of toxic waste; and sexually transmitted diseases.

Then I asked, "What is exciting about being your age and going into the world you are facing?" I expected a barrage of answers, but I got puzzled looks, coughs, and a few mumbled replies. I actually had to coach them to see the possibilities out there to be developed, discovered, and realized.

That experience was sobering and chilling. What had turned the star trek of those young people into a march through mud? The question is complex, but part of the answer lies in the fact they represent a generation that has grown up absorbing, on the average, from twelve thousand to fifteen thousand hours of television viewing. By the time they graduate from high school, they have watched thousands of rapes, robberies, and murders, some real and some imaginary. Combine the effects of TV advertising with the overwhelming emphasis on death, disaster, sex, and violence shown on TV news and dramatic programming, and you can begin to understand why young people feel they don't have much future.

While public and educational channels, as well as some cable networks, do their best to offer a healthy alternative, most of what is available on TV is junk food that leads to mental malnutrition and poor emotional and spiritual health. Television constantly exposes children and adults to antisocial behavior performed by the incompetent, the uncouth, and the insane. At the other extreme are the good-looking superheroes with unnatural strength and superhuman abilities. When average individuals compare themselves to their TV heroes, they usually see themselves as being grossly inadequate.

Recent studies have revealed that what we listen to and what we watch have a marked effect on our imaginations, our learning patterns, and our behaviors. First, we are exposed to new behaviors and characters. Next, we learn to imitate those new behaviors. In the last and most crucial step, we adopt those behaviors as our own.

One of the most critical aspects of human development is the influence of repeated viewing, listening, and verbalizing in shaping our lifestyles. The information goes in harmlessly, almost unnoticed, on a daily basis. We don't react to it at first. But we do react later, when we aren't able to realize the basis for our reactions. In other words, our value systems are being formed whether we realize it or not.

WHY DO SO MANY THINK, *IT'S NOT FOR ME?*

I mentioned earlier that we have multiple self-images. We have an imagined concept of whether or not we have the potential to succeed at any given task or activity. We write our scripts and tell ourselves, "I can do it" or "There is no way."

I talk to people about their potential and ask, "Can you see it for yourself? Can you imagine it?"

The response is often negative: "No, I can't. Maybe it's for you or them, but not for me."

"Why?" I ask.

And these are the answers I get too frequently: "Because I'm not good looking enough or talented enough." "I don't have the gift of gab. You're smooth; I'm not." "I'm too old, too fat, too slow," or too "something" that's a negative characteristic.

I think of a very capable young man who regularly delivers express packages to our office. He's depressed because he is sure he could do more with his life, but he is equally sure it just won't happen. He knows he'll always be driving that delivery truck. He has listened to many of my motivational tapes. They get him "up" for a while, but he slips back into his same rut of depression.

He is obviously college material, but he has never taken any aptitude tests or college courses. He has thought about going to college at night, but it seems there is not enough time. He just got off on the wrong foot. He is past twenty-five, and it's already all over for him. He missed it. He just wasn't in the right place to make the right entry at the right level. He didn't get off to a fast-enough start, and he'll never catch up.

I see this all the time. A stock clerk wants to be a rock 'n' roll star, but he remains a stock clerk. Why? There are other stock clerks who have gone on to become actors, lawyers, teachers, even owners of the businesses where they were stock clerks. In the case of the stock clerk who wants rock 'n' roll stardom, the question is obvious: "In what rock 'n' roll group are you singing in your spare time?" And too often the stock clerk answers, "Well, none right now. I work in this stupid job, and I'm so exhausted by the time I get home I don't have anything left."

I've had similar conversations with my children. They've told me they would like to do or be a certain thing, and I would say, "Are you doing it now anywhere? Do you try to do it on Saturdays? Are you doing it in your spare time up in your room? Are you writing about it? Are you talking to your friends about it? Are you obsessed with it?"

"BUT, DAD, I WANT TO BE A STAR!"

Let's imagine that your son approaches you and says, "Dad, I really want to become an actor."

So you say, "Fantastic! First, we'll see if you can find a job close to where people are acting. Then I suppose you'll want to enroll in an actors' workshop, and you'll probably try to get some bit parts somewhere in some of the neighborhood theaters. Is that what you're thinking of?"

"Oh, no, no. Dad, you don't understand," your son says. "I want to be a star. I want to be in a movie or write a song and record it and get a big break just like Michael J. Fox or Bruce Springsteen."

There's the problem. People—young and old—are not willing to investigate, invest, and persist. They want instant success, and they want it *now*. Among the many letters I have received asking for the key to success, I will never forget the one on the two-part form that gave me the writer's message and left a section for "please reply below."

Dear Dr. Waitley: Please tell me everything I need to know to become a top speaker, to record tapes, write books, and make a fortune. I'm in a hurry, so please use the bottom of this form for your answer and that will enable you to get it off to me right away. I need your answer immediately.

I dutifully filled up the bottom of the form with "WORK, WORK, WORK, WORK, WORK, WORK, WORK" until there was no more room to write.

WE AREN'T LAZY, JUST BADLY INFORMED

I really don't believe that people like the delivery truck driver or the urgent letter writer are just naturally lazy. Instead, they suffer from crippled potential. Their feedback keeps writing a negative script day by day, prompted by memories of what they have been told in childhood and fueled by the negative input they receive from a world that is often more critical than constructive.

One of my daughters tells me of a teacher in her high school who said to her class, "I was going to let you all do this, but you're too dumb to do it on your own, so *for this group only* I will personally read the instructions. I fully expect this group to do poorly on this exam. You don't have the discipline. You talk all the time. You are unkempt and unruly. You're one of the worst groups of students I have ever had. I fully expect there will be few passing grades. Now, here's your exam."

I wish I could say that this story is a rare exception and that most teachers, supervisors, and parents are far more encouraging and nurturing of the delicate self-images that sit before them. But I wonder. I wonder because I've heard about the history professor in a large midwestern university who is notorious for flunking nearly half of every class he teaches. Sure enough, every year, nearly half of the students fail because it is simply expected. That's just the way it is in his class. Yet the same students go on and do well with other teachers in the same subject areas.

These two examples come from education, but similar examples can be cited in sports, industry, anywhere people are influencing and programming others.

The power of significant others to warp and twist your self-image is indeed awesome. The good news is, you don't have to play the part of victim. You can rewrite your script and become the victor in the drama called life. *You are your own scriptwriter,* and the play is never finished, no matter what your age, position, or place in life. You do not have to believe the myth that says:

YOU'RE NOT GOOD ENOUGH; YOU'RE STUCK RIGHT WHERE YOU ARE

People from all walks of life have simply refused to let this lie become part of their thinking. Instead they have recognized the age-old truth:

WHAT YOU SEE IS WHO YOU'LL BE

A secretary from San Francisco becomes the three-time champion of the World's Fastest Typist Contest with a record-breaking 132.4 words per minute. Linda Williams thanks God for the ability and potential that He built into her at birth and shares her secrets of how she has developed that potential to its fullest. Obviously, she practices on her typewriter a great deal. But her "real secret" is that she "subconsciously types all the time." You might say that she types her own script in her head constantly.

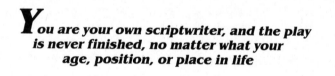

You are your own scriptwriter, and the play is never finished, no matter what your age, position, or place in life

✳

A homemaker picked up a tennis racket for the first time at the age of thirty-four. Eleven years later she had won eight national senior titles and doubles championships and was ranked #1 nationally in doubles and #7 in singles in the forty-and-over division.

Suella Bowden admits she relies more on God-given athletic ability than on tennis training. Many of her opponents learned tennis as children and have much smoother and purer strokes. She even admits that sometimes she "looks pretty funny" on the tennis court.

But she does not look so funny, thank you, when she steps up to accept the winner's trophy. She's a living, breathing, winning example of the truth that takes you beyond any myths you've been sold about your limitations. I'll state that truth one more time:

WHAT YOU SEE IS WHO YOU'LL BE

Do you really believe that? Or does it sound a little bit like another self-help success myth? In chapter 5 we'll look at one other crucial secret of how to see yourself and find your real potential. Your natural gifts lie deep inside, waiting for you to see them—perhaps for the first time.

FIVE ACTION STEPS TO A BETTER SELF-IMAGE

1. *Set your own internal standards* instead of comparing yourself to others. Accept yourself as you are right now, but keep upgrading your standards, lifestyle, behavior, professional training, and relationships by associating with winners.

2. *Project your best self.* Dressing well and looking your best do not have to involve trendy fashions and designer labels. Being appropriate for the occasion and being neat and clean are more important. Personal grooming and appearance provide an instantaneous projection on the surface of how you feel inside about yourself.

3. *Read a being-the-best biography each month.* Look for life stories of those who have reached the top in your profession or in your major hobby or of someone you admire. As you read, imagine yourself as the person you are reading about.

4. *Take stock this weekend of the images with which you display yourself.* Since the self-image comprises the visual, conceptual display of self-esteem (clothes, auto, home, garage, closets, dresser drawers, desk, photos, lawn, garden), make a priority list to get rid of all the clutter and sharpen up the expressions of your life.

5. *Go for a private walk* near the water, in the country, near the mountains, or to a park, and recall your childhood play and fantasies. What did you really love to do as a child? What were you good at? Which classes did you enjoy the most throughout your school years? If it weren't for time, money, or circumstance, what would you be doing with most of your days and nights? Dust off and reactivate your creativity.

CHAPTER 5

WILL THE "REAL" YOU PLEASE STAND UP___

IN THE MOVIE *Breaking Away* released some years ago, the story centers on a young man from Indiana who has grown up in a community and in a home where stonecutting is the only way to make a living. He comes to a crisis in his life when he tries to decide whether to consider trying to go to college. His SAT scores are good enough, and his application has been accepted. But he has deep reservations and self-doubt.

Everybody in his neighborhood is either a stonecutter by trade or the son or daughter of a stonecutter. Typically, the sons and daughters follow in their fathers' and mothers' career paths. It is tradition. They never go away to college. They stay close to home and cut stones.

The young man's father takes him to the university campus one day, and they stand on the front steps of the administration building.

"I cut the stones that you see placed here to build this university, Son," the father says, with his arm around his boy's shoulders. "I'm proud of that accomplishment. I think I did a good job." His son nods and they look each other in the eyes.

Then his father offers, "But I'm a cutter. And I've been watching you. You're not a cutter, and you don't have to try to be one. You can be anything you want. Just find out what you really like and what you really want, and you can be different. You can stand up and break away."

And so he does.

It's one thing to tell yourself or have someone else tell you that you can break away from the same old rut. But it's another thing to believe that what you see is who you'll be and let it make a real difference in your life. I constantly get letters that say in effect:

> Okay, Waitley, so my potential is tremendous. I don't have to live with all those limitations. I've heard all that before, but I'm stuck in the same dead-end job. What do I do first to get out of my rut? Do you know of any good positions for a person of my potential?

Such letters ask me to be practical—and specific. I don't know of any better way to do that than to respond, "Find out what you're good at."

THE SECRET TO FINDING ALL THAT POTENTIAL

An interesting and encouraging thing about potential is that we all have plenty of it, but it comes in different shapes and sizes. In addition to being given the gift of full value at birth, we all have certain personality traits and certain talents that are inborn. Some say we inherit these talents and traits. I like to call them our natural gifts.

In *Seeds of Greatness*, I discussed the book *Your Natural Gifts* by the late Margaret E. Broadley. She based her writing on the research efforts of the Human Engineering Laboratory of the Johnson O'Connor Research Foundation. I met Margaret in 1982 at a reception in Washington. She helped me understand more fully that winning and being the best are not strictly matters of attitude and perception. There must also be aptitude.

Through meeting Margaret, I became interested in the work of the Johnson O'Connor Research Foundation and took its battery of tests, which measure natural gifts in nineteen different areas. I shared my experience in *Seeds of Greatness* and was surprised by the number of letters that poured into my office from people who wanted to know more about the concept of finding your natural gifts.

In addition, thousands of the several hundred thousand readers wrote directly to the Johnson O'Connor Testing Centers for information. Many of them followed through to take the aptitude tests, the cost of which is significant but well worth the investment because they can give insights into individual potential better than any other tests I have seen. The following section briefly describes each test and the gift it identifies.

Personality determines if a person is "objective" (suited best for working with others) or "subjective" (more suited for specialized, individual work). Of the more than 600,000 clients tested in over sixty years by Johnson O'Connor, about three-fourths have revealed objective personalities.

Graphoria identifies clerical ability in dealing with figures and symbols. The test measures the ability to handle paperwork at high levels of speed and efficiency. Graphoria is necessary for bookkeeping, editing, secretarial tasks, and so on. It is also a real indicator of how well a person will do in school, where many subjects require this ability.

Ideaphoria indicates creative imagination or expression of ideas. It is extremely useful in fields such as sales, advertising, teaching, public relations, and journalism.

Structural visualization tests the ability to visualize solids and think in three dimensions. It is an aptitude possessed by concrete thinkers who don't do as well with abstract thinking. It is an absolutely critical skill for engineers, mechanics, and architects.

---

*I*t's not what you are that holds you back,
it's what you think you're not

✳

Inductive reasoning helps an individual form a logical conclusion from fragmented facts. This ability is important for lawyers, researchers, diagnostic physicians, writers, and critics—all of whom must be able to move quickly from the particular to the general pattern and see the big picture from all the details.

Analytical reasoning is useful for writers, editors, and computer programmers who need to organize concepts and ideas into sequences or classifications.

Finger dexterity is the ability to manipulate fingers skillfully. It is needed for any kind of manual or mechanical work. Secretaries need this skill for typing and for sorting papers.

Tweezers dexterity measures skill in handling small tools with precision. Surprisingly, there is little correlation between this skill and finger dexterity. Tweezers dexterity is vital for professionals such as surgeons and watch makers.

Observation is the ability to take careful notice. It is determined by showing a photo of a number of household objects and then showing ten other photos where at least one change has been made. The examinee must name the difference in each photograph. Observation is a useful skill for those engaged in research, particularly where noticing changes is important, for example, in the study of microscopic slides. It is also valuable for artists and painters.

Design memory tests how well someone can remember designs of all kinds. It is extremely helpful for anyone working with plans or blueprints.

The next four tests measure musical aptitude and ability. *Tonal memory* is the ability to remember sounds and express an ear for music. *Pitch discrimination* differentiates musical tones. *Rhythm memory* maintains rhythmic timing. *Timbre discrimination* distinguishes sounds of the same pitch and volume.

There are some other tests. *Number memory* is the ability to store many things in the mind at the same time. This aptitude is useful in many professions where it is necessary to call upon quantities of information and facts while making judgments, diagnoses, or determinations. It is useful for attorneys, physicians, and researchers.

Numerical reasoning is an aptitude for identifying relationships among sets of numbers. It is used in bookkeeping, computer programming, and actuarial work.

Silograms tests the ability to learn unfamiliar words and languages. This skill is extremely vital for translators, especially those employed at the United Nations. It is also important for speech teachers, language teachers, and persons doing written translation work. For example, Wycliffe Bible Translators, an independent missionary organization dedicated to translating the Bible into every known language on earth, has use for hundreds of people strong in this capability.

Foresight is the ability to keep the mind on a distant goal. Among the many occupations and professions that demand foresight would be market research analyst, sales forecaster, political scientist, diplomat, and politician. With all the talk about the clarity of hindsight, it is obvious that people in many walks of life lack this skill.

Color perception is the ability to distinguish colors. Some obvious professions where color perception is a necessity would be fashion design, painting, interior decorating, advertising, and any number of professions requiring art and layout functions.[1]

MOST OF US HAVE THREE TO FIVE APTITUDES

Few people tested by Johnson O'Connor have more than seven aptitudes and usually the number is three to five. When I took the tests, they confirmed that I am in the right profession—professional speaker and teacher on personal development and productivity—because of my strengths in ideaphoria, analytical reasoning, observation, and silograms.

The tests also revealed that I had natural talents related to music, such as tonal memory, pitch discrimination, and rhythm memory. Writing lyrics and songs comes naturally for me, but I have yet to develop any of my skills in this area.

I wasn't good at all in structural visualization, finger dexterity, design memory, and other areas related to engineering, mechanics, and high technology. Ironically enough, I went through high school with straight *A*'s and took many mathematical subjects because I knew my father had high hopes that I would attend one of the service academies. I managed to do well enough in subjects like math through sheer memory and good study habits, but this area has never been my natural gift.

Had I taken the Johnson O'Connor tests in high school, they would have shown that I could have done very well at a college or university while majoring in English, foreign language, music, the fine arts, writing, and speaking. Instead, I got out of high school and went into the Naval Academy at Annapolis where strong emphasis was put on the subjects of marine engineering, navigation, ordnance, and gunnery. I somehow struggled through my studies, graduated in the bottom half of my class, and went on to flight school where I had to do more struggling with subjects that I really wasn't gifted for.

I wound up flying a piece of high-tech equipment worth several million dollars, relying on my quick reflexes and my almost-photographic memory to get me through. I really didn't know how my aircraft operated. I couldn't take it apart and fix it. If the fire warning light had ever come on, my guess is that I would have steered it away from populated areas and then ejected, because I wouldn't have been able to figure out mechanically what was happening to cause the malfunction.

As far as natural gifts were concerned, my career with the navy was a classic example of flying by the seat of my pants. One of the major reasons I left the navy was my feeling that I wasn't in the right profession and I needed to develop natural gifts such as speaking and the communication of ideas. (I'll share more on this in chapter 6.)

FROM METER ASSEMBLY TO HUMAN ENGINEERING

Johnson O'Connor got started in aptitude testing in 1922 when he was just out of college. A Harvard graduate with a philosophy degree, he somehow found himself in charge of an engineering department in a General Electric plant in West Lynn, Massachusetts. The plant superintendent asked O'Connor to improve production in a meter assembly division, and he decided to do that by testing workers for manual dexterity. He reasoned that those who scored highest on the dexterity test would make better—and faster—assemblers.

O'Connor's manual dexterity test was not only successful in upping production; it also revealed that even with considerable practice, low scorers in dexterity could not bring their speed up to that of workers who scored high in the first place. O'Connor started to do more thinking and experimenting with aptitude tests. Was there a way to apply scientific testing to human abilities and relate those abilities to jobs and careers? Was there a way to scientifically measure the traits of people in various professions and identify traits that made those people successful?

The next test O'Connor developed measured powers of observation, and it was used to screen applicants for inspector jobs in the plant. O'Connor kept adding other tests for other abilities, and the demand became so great that he was soon doing a thriving business out of his home on evenings and weekends. Eventually, he set up shop at the Massachusetts Institute of Technology where he did aptitude testing for three years. Then he opened the Human Engineering Laboratory of the Johnson O'Connor Research Foundation.

O'Connor's long and brilliant career ended in 1973 when he and his wife journeyed to Mexico to test the aptitudes of primitive Zapotec Indians. While there, they contracted a disease that claimed both their lives.

The foundation continues O'Connor's work through sixteen testing centers located across the United States. The kind of testing done is particularly useful for helping people make career transitions or changes. One of their best services is to show people why they may be frustrated and unhappy because of being in the wrong kind of work. And this testing can open up new frontiers that people haven't thought about before.

FROM PERSONNEL WORK TO NICE 'N SPICY

For example, at age forty-one, Jane Leader had a good position in personnel work, but she was restless. She took the Johnson O'Connor tests, and after learning the results, she quit her job and started her own business. The nine hours of testing had revealed that she was more objective than 96 percent of all people ever tested by the foundation. That meant she really enjoyed dealing with people, a natural skill for managing a store or other kind of business. Jane also showed high graphoria, the ability to deal with numbers and details, something that would stand her in good stead as a business manager.

Choosing a likely location in a busy mall, she opened a shop called Nice 'n Spicy, where she specialized in herbs, spices, coffees, teas, and handcrafts. The shop was a great success, and after only a year, she started offering franchises for similar shops in other locations. How does Jane feel about finding her natural gifts? "For the first time," she says with a big smile, "I'm really happy in my work!"

Another odyssey of natural gifts was made by Helen Vogel who graduated from high school in 1970 and went on to Stanford to study economics and anthropology. While still in college, she took the Johnson O'Connor tests and found that she was a highly structural as well as a subjective personality. She was told she would probably succeed in a profession such as engineering.

She didn't take the advice to heart, however, and switched her major to English and creative writing. After graduation, she worked in a bookstore and a student loan office, but she found little satisfaction. In a little over two years, she reentered school to pursue an engineering program. She earned her engineering degree and joined a firm where she works enthusiastically on predicting and reducing noise levels in buildings. Helen is extremely happy with engineering as a profession, but she still takes a strong interest in liberal arts by writing short stories, playing the piano, and taking art classes.[2]

In another case, a young woman who had failed miserably in her chosen profession of teaching came to a testing center to learn why her dream had shattered. She had always been good with children, but in the classroom everything fell apart. For some reason, the discipline in her class was the worst in the whole school, and she had a terrible time trying to get the children to learn anything.

Her tests showed she had aptitudes precisely opposite those of a good teacher. Instead of being highly objective, a much-needed trait for teaching, she was extremely subjective. In addition, she scored very low in ideaphoria and inductive reasoning, two other vital traits for teaching. Her tests showed her with 100 percent structural visualization, and she left the center in high spirits, determined to start a new career as a lab technician or possibly an engineer.[3]

HOW AN ENTIRE SCHOOL FOUND ITS GIFTS

The potential for the Johnson O'Connor tests to help schools do a better job is tremendous. Lake Grove School, located on Long Island, New York, has employed Johnson O'Connor testing for all its pupils with fascinating results.

For example, Bonnie, an otherwise very bright student, could not learn chemistry. The tests revealed that she had no structural visualization, something absolutely necessary for chemistry. Bonnie tested high in abstract visualization, which would help her with the subjects of history and government, but she was still sure she was stupid because chemistry was such a mystery.

Jeff was the opposite of Bonnie. Give him a test tube, a Bunsen burner, and some charts, and he'd salivate. Put him in a history or geography class, and he'd sleep or daydream. Jeff was high in structural visualization and very low on abstract thinking. History, dates, and philosophy were boring and confusing for him.

Gayle always did her homework, and though she took a little longer than the other students, she still did a good job. She could answer all the questions in class, but during a test, she totally collapsed. Teachers knew her grades didn't reflect her knowledge, but they were baffled about what to do.

Johnson O'Connor testing revealed Gayle had low graphoria, a slowness of speed at changing symbols into ideas and ideas into symbols. Low-graphoria students generally don't do well on timed tests or math computation.

Frank struggled through Spanish for almost two years before he discovered that he was very poor in silograms. It didn't comfort him a great deal to know that 50 percent of the population suffers from low silograms (inability to learn a foreign language), but after he took the tests, at least he knew what the problem was.

To cope with the different aptitudes of the pupils, Lake Grove breaks down courses according to structural or abstract. Classes with high-structure students have high-structure teachers, and classes with high-abstract students have high-abstract teachers. Not surprisingly, teachers and students get along beautifully because they have similar perceptions and ways of doing things.

Low-graphoria students are given other kinds of work to test their intelligence. For example, instead of having to compute math problems, they might be given a project or a multimedia exercise. Math students with low graphoria are also allowed to use pocket calculators when possible.

Foreign languages are no longer required at Lake Grove. They have been replaced by social studies courses, which cover culture and conversational language to enable students to function in a mobile, multilingual world.

Principal Michael DeSisto observed that aptitudes are not good or bad, they are just aptitudes. They simply say what a student can find difficult or easy. He commented, "With the help of the aptitude tests, we are better able to determine the place to start from, the road to take, the best way to move along that road."[4]

VOCABULARY—KEY TO YOUR SUCCESS

Of key importance at Lake Grove is vocabulary. Students are tested to find individual levels in relation to other children of the same age and grade. Very personal programs in reading and writing are designed to help students raise vocabulary levels.

According to Johnson O'Connor personnel, vocabulary is a key skill needed for success in today's highly competitive world. Unlike other aptitudes, vocabulary is one capability that can be improved with effort and discipline.

As Johnson O'Connor developed his first batteries of aptitude tests in the early years of his work, he and his associates discovered a distinct correlation between vocabulary and career success. A limited vocabulary can definitely affect career progress. People with excellent gifts and abilities often fail to develop them because of their lack of vocabulary and inability to communicate.

Do you wonder about the cause of the much-publicized drop in SAT (college entrance) test scores in recent years? The Johnson O'Connor Foundation records show that vocabulary skills of eighteen-year-olds have dropped dramatically between 1955 and 1980.

The Johnson O'Connor staff reports that the difference between an excellent vocabulary and a mediocre one is only 3,500 words. Their centers provide several different books for those who want to improve vocabulary levels. Says a Johnson O'Connor pamphlet: "The aptitudes point which direction a person should go; the vocabulary level predicts how far a person will go in his or her chosen career."

It is no surprise that Johnson O'Connor surveys show that successful people usually have excellent vocabularies. To be the best, develop your vocabulary and word skills. Your success ratio will increase in all arenas of life. You will be able to communicate your feelings and goals and not be misunderstood as often. You will write better letters and be a more interesting conversationalist. Instead of groping for words, you will have them on the tip of your tongue, ready to serve your purposes and bring out your abilities.

HIGH SCHOOL IS THE BEST TIME TO BE TESTED

The earlier you can find your natural gifts, the better. However, whether you are sixteen or sixty, it's never to late to uncover who you really are. The Johnson O'Connor tests have been given to children as young as nine, but they are probably most effective at age sixteen or seventeen when high-school students are making college or career choices.

My wife Susan has taken the tests as have all six of our children. The results have often been startling, sometimes surprising, and always interesting. Will my sons follow in my footsteps to the speaking podium? Actually, my daughters are more gifted in this area while my sons have found their own special gifts that they are developing.

I often wish that some of my older children had been tested a lot sooner. In many ways I missed noticing their natural gifts. For example, I would have picked one of our daughters to be a veterinarian because of her love for animals. She turned out to be one of the best speakers among all the children.

The son I thought might be a pro athlete is headed for marketing or sales. The son I was sure would become a serious researcher is developing opportunities in broadcasting.

And so it has gone. The Johnson O'Connor testing revealed that I had pegged many of our children wrong, which simply proves to me that parents can't really do enough to help their children discover their gifts. Too often parents hand over the job to a high-school counselor who has two hundred or more students to advise. The counseling that is done is based on their report cards and some casual conversations about upward mobility and career patterns. And then the students go home and too often hear at the dinner table something like this: "Why don't you go where the money is—the computer field is wide open."

Check what you say to children, and never say anything unless you can encourage or support them

---
✳

A problem in today's society is that parents really have little opportunity to help children discover natural gifts. Contemporary culture and lifestyle leave very little time to spend really getting to know children by watching them and working with them.

In the "old days" children often worked on the farm or in the family business right alongside mom and dad. Now they run from school to Little League to Brownies to dancing class and, finally, to bed. And about all that mom and dad get, if they are lucky, are brief reports on how things are going. In many cases only mom hears the terse grunts of, "Okay, I guess," as she chauffeurs the kids from one activity to another. Dad doesn't get home on the seven o'clock commuter until after they're fast asleep or in the middle of a sitcom.

Because they are "blessed" with all these wonderful activities and opportunities, children grow up having only a vague idea of what they are good at—sports, ballet, math, for example—but for the most part, all this is kept in the context of going to school or being part of the team or club. It is seldom directly related to a possible career.

Thus, young people reach college age and beyond still unsure of what they want to do in life. Young adults talk about finding themselves, but they aren't sure where to look. Meanwhile, the parents sit by, wringing their hands and worrying about young Steve. Here he is, twenty-nine years old. Will he ever get a job?

Steve's potential is in there somewhere, awaiting discovery and development. Parents can do a lot to help children discover natural gifts. But whatever they do, they should not imitate the father of the eight-year-old Little Leaguer who struck out all the time. The dad bought the boy a soccer ball and presented it to him saying, "Obviously, you're no good in baseball. Maybe you just need a bigger ball—something you can kick around."

Parents and significant others, such as coaches and teachers, can encourage or squelch a child's unique potential. Check what you say, and never say anything unless it can have a note of encouragement and support.

If I had my life to live over with our children, I would get them tested no later than their sixteenth birthday by the Johnson O'Connor Research Foundation. With the results of those tests in mind, I would be particularly interested in their specific abilities and would introduce them to many experiences that would give them opportunities to develop their natural gifts and interests. I would try everything: eating in different ethnic restaurants, going to hear string quartets, taking in local theater productions as well as off-Broadway shows, if possible.

Children will always be influenced by radio and television and, of course, their peer group. They will always want to go to the "oingo, boingo" concerts, but along with those diversions, parents should try to give them broader experiences that just might strike a deeper chord within.

I meet many parents who doubt that they have much impact on their children. I tell them not to be fooled by the mythical generation gap that is supposed to keep kids and adults in two different worlds. If any gaps form between parents and children, it's because parents chose to take the easy way out and let the children go their own way.

Make allowances for their personal tastes, but in addition to things like rock concerts, be sure they have opportunities to see or hear *Man of La Mancha* or a local string quartet or a touring college choir. Let them take a friend along, for moral support. You may not get much positive feedback, but inside, they can be thinking, *That was neat—a lot neater than I thought it would be.*

Try a lot of things. Spend more money on experience and less on toys and other material possessions that are supposed to enhance life or somehow vicariously substitute for it. Isn't it ironic that we spend more at Christmas on toys than we spend the rest of the year on giving our children interesting experiences? We try to buy their love with birthday and Christmas presents when we could give them the priceless gift of discovering the unlimited potential they have within themselves.

Although I have devoted much of this chapter to the Johnson O'Connor Aptitude Testing Program, I want to put in a cautionary note: it would be inadvisable to put any person's choice of career totally in the aptitude testing basket. I agree that testing for natural ability is extremely important, but to find the ideal career, the individual also needs to acquire training and experience and, if possible, observe some good role models or mentors.

If you can discover your natural abilities early on, it may give you a tremendous boost toward developing your life along the paths of greatest potential and fulfillment. But even if you aren't able to do that, it's never too late. Stanley Spiro, featured in a story in *Time* magazine, is a case in point.

HOW A DENTIST GOT "IN THE MOOD"

Stan Spiro trained in dentistry at Temple University, and while in college, he picked up extra money by playing alto sax, clarinet, or flute in any band that would have him. Apparently, a lot of bands did, and during his college days, he played briefly with Glenn Miller and Jack Teagarden, to name just two. Following graduation, he abandoned his musical interests and concentrated on dentistry and anesthesiology for thirty-eight years. In addition to his work in a dentist's office, Stan wrote two books: *Amensia-Analgesia, Techniques in Dentistry* and *Pain and Anxiety Control in Dentistry*, both of which sound light years away from getting "In the Mood" with Glenn Miller.

When Stan turned sixty-five, he retired from dentistry and moved with his wife, Thelma, to Florida. He tried kicking back on Marco Island, a windswept bit of paradise in the Gulf of Mexico, but he soon started humming "Don't Get Around Much Anymore." Those musical gifts that had been used only occasionally over the years at odd moments came bubbling to the surface, and Stan decided to start his own big band.

He put together Stan Spiro and the Townsmen Orchestra, which features music in the Glenn Miller mood. His musicians include a retired oral surgeon, a librarian, a retired railroad dispatcher, two high-school students, a newspaper publisher, a marina owner, an embroidery manufacturer, a high-school music teacher, a florist, a racing car manufacturer, and several sales representatives. The band vocalist is the manager of a condominium project.

Stan rehearsed the band for what seemed like ages before taking it public. It was soon the toast of southwestern Florida and was booked for months in advance in nightclubs, country clubs, banquets, benefits— anywhere it was invited to charm nostalgia buffs with numbers like "These Things Remind Me of You."

The Glenn Miller sound is perfect for the age group the musicians cater to, which is just about everybody older than a teenager. They don't do it for the money; they do it because they love it. For Stan Spiro, retirement is truly a dream. In fact, it's one long "Moonlight Serenade."[5]

Stan Spiro is only one example of someone who found a natural gift and enjoyed it. You don't have to wait until retirement. I know of a forty-nine-year-old woman who reentered the business world after a quarter of a century as a homemaker. She sold $750,000 in real estate the first year. There was also a jack-of-all-trades who had been a bartender, health technician, soldier, and salesman; he went into a new career combining management, data processing, and engineering.

Stories pop up every day about highly paid executives who take a cut in income of anywhere from one-third to one-half but achieve self-fulfillment with their own business, ranch, or farm.

These examples of natural gift odysseys are powerful evidence to refute the crippling myths about limitations and not having what it takes, which we looked at in chapter 4. It is all too easy to let these lies keep you living in Pity City, neglecting your potential, lamenting your fate. Don't listen to the myth:

YOU CAN'T FIGHT CITY HALL; YOU'RE A VICTIM OF THE SYSTEM

I have never really met the mythical inhabitants of the "City Hall" that is supposed to be perpetuating this massive conspiracy against your potential and mine. That's because City Hall is as imaginary as the limitations that you or others may be placing on your real potential. The truth, which Johnson O'Connor or any reputable aptitude testing firm can reveal, is this:

YOUR NATURAL GIFTS ARE THE KEY TO FULFILLING YOUR POTENTIAL FOR SUCCESS

Find your natural gifts. Develop them. Then use them to be the best you can be!

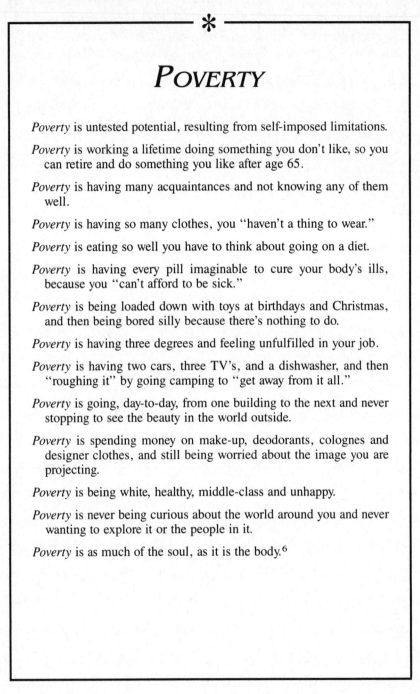

POVERTY

Poverty is untested potential, resulting from self-imposed limitations.

Poverty is working a lifetime doing something you don't like, so you can retire and do something you like after age 65.

Poverty is having many acquaintances and not knowing any of them well.

Poverty is having so many clothes, you "haven't a thing to wear."

Poverty is eating so well you have to think about going on a diet.

Poverty is having every pill imaginable to cure your body's ills, because you "can't afford to be sick."

Poverty is being loaded down with toys at birthdays and Christmas, and then being bored silly because there's nothing to do.

Poverty is having three degrees and feeling unfulfilled in your job.

Poverty is having two cars, three TV's, and a dishwasher, and then "roughing it" by going camping to "get away from it all."

Poverty is going, day-to-day, from one building to the next and never stopping to see the beauty in the world outside.

Poverty is spending money on make-up, deodorants, colognes and designer clothes, and still being worried about the image you are projecting.

Poverty is being white, healthy, middle-class and unhappy.

Poverty is never being curious about the world around you and never wanting to explore it or the people in it.

Poverty is as much of the soul, as it is the body.[6]

CHAPTER 6

*T*HE ROAD BEST-TRAVELED

CHARLIE BROWN, THE lovable star of Charles Schultz's *Peanuts* cartoons, is possibly at his best when he teaches us truths from the pitcher's mound. Charlie is captain and manager of the famed Peanuts Baseball Team, which usually loses 0–176. But Charlie isn't discouraged. He knows his team has what it takes—the players just have to keep trying.

"Ah, yes," Charlie sighs as another line drive whistles past his ear headed for the center-field fence. "It's tough to bear the awesome burden of permanent potential!"

Once again Charlie's comment rings true. You know you have potential and natural gifts in there somewhere, but unless you develop them, you will be cursed with that same awesome burden. To avoid being in a state of permanent potential, you must find the road best suited for you. It may not be the road most traveled, that yellow brick road to the lifetime bonanza you hope to encounter. What you seek is the road best traveled so that you will be challenged to be all you can be.

It took me until my early thirties to realize my potential and develop a self-image to match. My natural gifts were evident very early. When I was just a small boy, I would go down the block to a neighbor's home and recite a poem or sing "I'm An Ol' Cowhand" for the price of a cookie. Mrs. Door, the woman who lived just two houses down, the Beardsleys across the street on the corner, and all the others I knew on the block would wait for the little cowhand to come by to give his speech, recite his poem, or sing his song. And I did it without being coached or taught because I enjoyed it. Besides, I could get cookies that way. I liked getting rewards.

In grammar school I found that I could remember things and repeat them without much effort. I was much better at saying things and talking than I was at drawing, computing, or figuring out. Besides liking to sing, I was very good at describing events verbally. It was fun to raise my hand and give the answers. I just plain liked to hear the sound of my own voice!

When I got to junior high and high school, I sampled as much of life as possible. I won varsity letters in baseball, but due to my lack of height and weight, I had to settle for junior varsity football and B basketball for the shorter kids. Unlike the stereotype of the athlete who supposedly never cracks a book, I liked to study. I really enjoyed English, creative writing, and foreign languages, and I also found time to take part in school plays and sing in the choral group.

Throughout high school, I kept talking and entertaining whenever I could. I ran for school offices and won. You might say I had a gift of gab.

MY FAMILY NURTURED MY SPECIAL GIFT

My mother encouraged me to be a reader and to express myself in writing. Like most moms, she would always make a big to-do over my poetry and my singing. She attended my games and my plays at school. She even helped me with campaign speeches when I ran for student body president.

My mother wrote poetry, and she would often read aloud some bits of verse she had done. She got her love of writing and books from her mother who worked for forty years as a proofreader at a major printing and publishing company in San Diego. Grandma loved the printed word. You could say that next to her family, it was her entire life. Over those four decades she read thousands of brochures, manuals, and books.

In addition, my grandfather owned a stationery store and a book bindery, and he loved collecting books. It is easy to see where my mother got her love of reading, communicating, and using the imagination. While my father was away serving in the merchant marine during World War II, Mom single-handedly took care of me, my brother, and my sister. She kept the family going and planted seeds of self-expression in me that would spring up and bear fruit many years later.

As much as I loved Mom and Grandma, my father had a very special relationship with me. Dad was a singularly handsome man, the son of a Bolivian mother and a Scotch-Welsh father. After spending several years at sea in the merchant marine, he devoted most of the rest of his life to being a service department representative at a local Buick agency in San Diego. He was the man who would greet people when they drove up to have their cars serviced. He would fill out the form, smile, and say, "We'll have it ready by five o'clock."

My dad was always in a good mood, and he always saw life as opening and expanding. There is little question that he was the model from whom I learned to memorize and recite sizable portions of material. Every night he and I teamed up to do the dishes together after Mom and my sister had made supper. As we worked, Dad would quote from memory long passages of *Don Quixote* in flawless Spanish as I dried plates, pots, and pans and listened in awe.

I grew up wanting to please my father, and I have always fondly remembered the special good-night times we had together when he was home instead of away at sea. Bedtime offers some marvelous moments for parents to deal with children. It can be a time for real communication.

While rearing my own children, I've always tried to use bedtime the way Dad did—to communicate rather than simply terminate the evening with a terse, "Okay, time for bed." When Dad came in my bedroom to tuck me in, nothing interfered with our communication and sharing; it was our special time. Dad would say in various ways, "I want you to know that you are the most special human being I've ever been privileged to know, and I am proud to wear your name."

YOU CAN BE A PRISONER OR A PIONEER

As I got older, my father would play word games with me. One of our favorites was to see how many combinations we could get out of the letters *POW*. A standard definition of POW is "prisoner of war," but it can also mean "prince of Wales" or "power of women." If you don't like your job, it can mean "prisoner of work" or "prisoner of wishes." If you have a weak vocabulary and have trouble communicating, it can mean "prisoner of words."

The point is, you are a prisoner in a world of your own making. How you imagine and perceive your world is the world you will live in. You can be a prisoner or a pioneer. Dad used to say, "See the world as open and abundant. You're going to go a long way, Son. I expect you to succeed. I expect you to have a great life."

DAD'S MAGNIFICENT OBSESSION

Because of his background in the merchant marine, Dad loved to talk about the day I would attend the academy at Annapolis or West Point. We listened to radio broadcasts of the Army-Navy football games and thrilled to the exploits of Felix "Doc" Blanchard (Mr. Inside) and Glen Davis (Mr. Outside).

On my seventeenth birthday, a week before graduating from high school, I joined the Naval Reserve, which gave me future eligibility to take the entrance exams for the U.S. Naval Academy. We tend to live up to our own expectations as well as the expectations of significant others. Sometimes, as I found out years later, the deliberate or unconscious pressures from well-meaning parents or other important peers can push us into an educational or job situation that doesn't fit us or our abilities. My dad wanted the best for me, but what we didn't know at the time was that his dream and my natural gifts didn't fit together.

After graduating from high school, I studied every night for a year to ready myself for competitive exams against several hundred other young men from my district who were interested in getting an appointment to Annapolis. It was a major undertaking that became an obsession. I was totally committed to getting that appointment. I took the exams and did well. I wrote to congressmen. I wrote to senators. Finally, the appointment came through, and in June of 1951 I boarded a Greyhound bus in San Diego to travel to Annapolis, Maryland, and began my new career with the United States Navy.

I arrived at Annapolis and began my career as a lowly plebe among 3,700 other midshipmen. Back in my high-school pond, I had been a great white shark: a varsity letterman, a straight *A* student, student body president, and something of a golden-tongued orator. My *A*'s were legitimate in the subjects of English, foreign language, and history, where I had natural gifts. In the science and math courses, I managed *A*'s but only with the greatest efforts and a persuasive tongue that helped me talk my teachers into upping *B*'s and *B* + 's to *A*'s.

At Annapolis I was one of 1,200 in the plebe class. *Everybody* there had been a student body president, a good athlete, and a straight *A* student. At Annapolis the instructors weren't too interested in honing my skills in English, foreign languages, literature, and history. They wanted me to zero in on math, engineering, science, and navigation.

The great white shark from La Jolla High School soon felt like a guppy who had wandered into a school of hungry largemouth bass. The competition wasn't just fierce, it was overwhelming. Because I needed every minute of cram time I could get just to keep up, I studied in bed under the covers with a flashlight after "lights out" at 10:15 P.M. Had the officers, who made hourly checks of our quarters, caught me, I would have been put on report, but I took the chance. For four years I struggled with the math, science, and engineering courses and achieved the dubious distinction of scoring in the lower half of my class throughout my career as a midshipman.

My self-image was saved from total annihilation because I managed to excel in after-dinner speaking (something all midshipmen had to do) and in writing musical shows for the Naval Academy's really fine drama and musical theater group. If it hadn't been for those high points, all four years at the academy would have been grim indeed.

THE NIGHT ED SULLIVAN CAUGHT MY ACT

I recall writing, producing, and directing a very successful musical show during my senior year. The admirals liked it. The chief of naval operations liked it. Ed Sullivan even came down, watched, and liked it. He put a small piece of it on his show. At that point my production was the clearest indication of what I was really good at.

The navy wanted me to be good at engineering, navigation, ocean sciences, running boilers and the like. But I was really good at what I called my hobby. I've talked with many other people who have found the same thing to be true. An extracurricular activity—the thing they call a hobby—is really a natural gift and what they do best. Sometimes people can turn hobbies into careers. Sometimes it doesn't work out, but it's worth considering the possibilities. Are your hobbies really what you do best? Should you be thinking about trying to turn your hobby into a vocation?

Take a good look at the things you love to do on weekends, the things you're looking forward to doing when you retire. These hobbies just may be your natural gifts that are lying dormant but waiting to be fully developed. Perhaps there is a way to take your natural hobby skills and incorporate them into your current job to make it more meaningful and worthwhile.

I believe that a job is simply a description of certain duties. Your job can always be filled by someone else. You test this theory at least once a year when you take a vacation. What is important is to bring to your job your talents, hobbies, skills, and joy of working. Contrary to popular belief, a job doesn't really offer you opportunity. *You* are the opportunity, and you bring that opportunity—your natural gifts, potential, and purpose—to the job.

I was graduated from Annapolis in 1955, and I faced a choice. I could become a line officer aboard ship (the black-shoe navy) or a line officer as a pilot (the brown-shoe navy). I chose flight school at Pensacola, Florida, and there I trained to become a carrier-based navy attack pilot. Despite my poor showing in the classroom at Annapolis, I did quite well as a pilot by counting on my quick natural reflexes and being willing to take risks.

I grew to love flying. I loved making the high-speed, low-level runs and landing tons of hurtling metal on a bobbing carrier deck in a rough sea. That little kid who would go down the block to sing a verse of "I'm An Ol' Cowhand" for a cookie was still inside wanting to get out, but I was too busy trying to develop what I thought was to be my career to pay attention to that part of myself.

But then my life took a very slight turn in a significant new direction. I was asked to serve as a public affairs officer. One of the major events for which I was responsible was the Naval Air Gunnery Meet, which was held annually to see who was top gun. After coming out of flight school and qualifying for carrier duty, I had done pretty well as a top gun myself, so it was no surprise that I enjoyed handling the press relations for the event.

The gunnery meet of 1957 was a great success. In fact, I liked handling PR so well I went to the commander in charge of public information of the Naval Air Pacific Fleet and told him I wanted to join his staff. He told me, "You can try to do that, Waitley, but you'll ruin your career. Your career is set. You're a line officer, and your job is to go to sea and fly planes, not talk about them. My advice to you is to go ahead and do just that."

Reluctantly, I decided he was right. My natural gifts and real potential had to be subdued and put aside while I followed my "career path." My only career opportunity with the navy had to do with flying planes. Flying was exciting and it was something I could do quite well, but I knew that deep down it wasn't totally fulfilling to me. Speaking and communicating—my natural gifts—were what I really wanted to pursue, but I would have to do them "on the side" as my hobby. Without realizing it, I bought into a myth accepted by many people who wind up in jobs that they do quite adequately but that don't really satisfy:

YOU'VE MADE YOUR CAREER CHOICE; NOW LIVE WITH IT

Today, of course, I realize this myth does not have to control my life—or yours. I spend most of my waking moments trying to convince people in all kinds of careers that it's worth it to risk following a dream:

LET YOUR NATURAL GIFTS—WHAT YOU LOVE TO DO—
TAKE YOU WHERE YOU REALLY WANT TO GO

Following the gunnery meet, I had to wait for deployment to a squadron. Because a squadron wasn't immediately available, the navy decided to give me TAD (Temporary Additional Duty). The commander in chief of the Korean navy, Admiral Yung Woon Lee had just arrived in the country and was on his way to Washington to meet with our naval high command. He had come to ask for additional support from the U.S. Navy Department.

My superiors felt that with all my PR experience I was a likely choice to accompany Admiral Lee on his travels. Since Lieutenant Waitley liked to relate and talk, here was his chance until they could find him a carrier and get him back to his career.

I reported for duty with some misgivings but soon found Admiral Lee to be a brilliant and personable gentleman. For a five-star officer, he was unusually informal. He had spent quite a bit of time in the States and spoke fluent English.

I tried to keep proper protocol, but in no time at all we became rather good friends. When he talked to me in private, it wasn't the admiral and the lieutenant junior grade; it was Lee and Waitley discussing life, goals, dreams, and plans. Like today's NFL coach turned sportscaster, John Madden, Admiral Lee and I traveled by train. Unlike Madden, the admiral liked to fly, but he just loved the opportunity to see America up close.

One day as we were going from Denver to Chicago, he asked me, "If you could do anything, what would you do for your navy?"

I answered that I was very concerned about the way the navy communicated its role and mission to the public and the Congress. It seemed to me that the air force was getting too much of the budget and the more positive coverage in the press. The navy was a bit too conservative, not very aggressive in promoting or advancing the "romance of the seas."

"Then why don't you do that?" he asked. "Why don't you become the navy's #1 spokesman?"

I answered that I couldn't. "The navy has spent hundreds of thousands of dollars to make me into a pilot. I've made a commitment. My path is set. The navy has been good to me. I can't let down the people who have trained me and had faith in me to do what *I* signed up to do."

"Well, I don't know," he mused. "Do you think you can be effective if you're doing what you really don't like to do?"

The answer was fairly obvious. You can't effectively use your real potential if you're not doing what you're best at, what you really like and enjoy. That is why you work. You don't work for the money; you work to be able to use your talent and natural gifts in the way you know they should be used.

And then our conversation took a turn that I now believe reset my life course and purpose. Admiral Lee wanted to know what I liked about flying. I explained that I liked overcoming fear while doing something difficult well. "I like the risk mixed with the thrill of being up there in the clouds, feeling closer to God," I said.

---

*If you don't stand for something,
you'll fall for anything*

✳

"Very noble," the admiral observed. "And how do you feel about getting catapulted off the deck of a carrier in the middle of the night in a storm and maybe having to go blow up a bridge or an ammunition depot? Let's face it, Waitley, you've got the wrong reasons for doing what you're doing. You really want to help people and show them why and how they can be better. Instead of defending your country, you'd rather be promoting it."

Admiral Lee had me. I knew he was right, but I was still stuck. My die was cast, and my course was set. Like a true navy man, I had to sail to the port that had been chosen for me.

MY CAREER COLLIDES WITH 31-KNOT BURKE

And so we arrived in Washington, D.C., and were ushered into the office of Admiral Arleigh Burke, the chief of naval operations and the #1 flag officer in the United States Navy. He was a black-shoe navy man who had the distinction of being known as 31-knot Burke, a nickname he had picked up while commanding a destroyer he took into battle at thirty-one knots, or "full speed ahead." Thirty-one knots doesn't sound very fast for ships today, but back in World War II and Korean War days, doing thirty-one knots on the sea was something like breaking the sound barrier. Arleigh Burke was the black-shoe navy's version of Chuck Yeager.

Admiral Burke eyed my navy wings coolly and grunted a greeting. I got the feeling I should have taken my leave and waited outside the door. Most black-shoe navy men were not fond of fly boys, whom they perceived as somewhat arrogant—the country club set.

Then he turned to Admiral Lee, took a long puff on his pipe, and asked, "What can I do for you?"

The Korean commander in chief discussed ways in which the United States and Korea could cooperate more effectively in maintaining peace and the balance of seapower in the face of continuing North Korean belligerence. Admiral Lee had a list of technical and manpower requests he hoped our Chief of Naval Operations would support.

Admiral Burke looked at the list and commented that he thought it could be arranged. Congress still had memories of the Korean War and was always interested in helping our allies maintain a strong defense. Then he looked up: "Anything else?"

"Oh, there is one other thing," Admiral Lee threw in as an afterthought. "My friend here, Lieutenant Waitley, is interested in public relations. He thinks the air force is getting most of the glory and the budget because the navy's a little too laid back, conservative, and stodgy. He'd like to promote the navy against the air force, and after spending a few weeks with him, I think he'd be a good man for the job."

Admiral Burke's pipe gave a couple of puffs like a destroyer revving up to thirty-one knots, and he swung around to eye me steadily through the smoke. I felt myself shrinking before his gaze, but somehow there didn't seem to be room enough to hide under his ashtray. With irritation in his voice he said, "We can probably arrange for some kind of transfer."

Admiral Lee and I parted soon after that interview with Admiral Burke. I thanked him for trying to help me, and he went back to Korea thinking that he had done me a great favor. Actually, he had, but it would take a while for me to realize it. At first it seemed as if my naval career was basically ruined. In no time at all, I was transferred to Washington to "fly a desk."

My new job title was Assistant Head of Media Relations and Special Projects for the Navy Department. My assignment was to help the U.S. Navy Recruiting Service convince civilians that joining the navy would be a romantic, popular, and pleasant way to serve their country.

At first, flying a desk was great fun. I wore civilian clothes, traveled freely, and was soon working with big names in the entertainment field. To promote the navy's recruiting campaign, I helped arrange an appearance on TV for the Naval Academy Glee Club with Fred Waring and The Pennsylvanians. I also helped put the Naval Aviation Cadet Choir on the "Perry Como Show." And I even managed to help convince the Ice Capades to put in a routine that featured four skaters in sleek blue costumes simulating a high-speed, precision-flying formation by the Blue Angels.

In addition, we made "Sea Power" films for high schools and colleges to promote the idea of preserving a strong navy and a strong country. Those videos were some of the first of their kind, featuring sailors answering the call to General Quarters and fliers zooming in to stop on a dime on carrier decks. The navy had never looked more exciting, and enlistment statistics had seldom looked better.

One of the features I enjoyed most about my job was getting to know young celebrities such as Jimmy Rogers, Connie Francis and, of course, Perry Como. Another young fellow I met was Pat Boone; his white buck shoes were just becoming a trademark in the late fifties and early sixties. I recall attending a national disc jockey convention in Miami, Florida, and going swimming with Pat Boone in a special roped-off area. No, his manager wasn't worried about sharks; he just wanted to keep Pat from being mobbed by the young girls who were hanging on the ropes ready to pounce on him!

My life seemed full. At last it appeared that I was able to use my natural gifts and pursue my first love. But with all the glamor and excitement, I still had a big empty space inside. I saw myself in a total dilemma. I was a lieutenant in the United States Navy, capable of piloting some of the most advanced aircraft in the world, but I spent my days wearing civilian clothes and flying to my next PR appointment.

Physically, I was quite able to fly high-tech airplanes very well, but instead I was flying a desk. It was beginning to look as if my courage might be in question. Yes, I thought I was doing what I loved to do—media work and public relations—but in the navy, at that time, a man had to have poor eyesight or some other problem to be a fully qualified pilot and wind up doing something else for any extended period of time. Certainly, public relations work was no long-term job for a naval aviator who was an Annapolis graduate.

I LOVED THE NAVY, I LOVED TO FLY, BUT . . .

I started thinking about resignation. The phrase "mixed emotions" doesn't begin to describe how that felt. I knew I would severely disappoint and hurt my dad whom I loved deeply. I loved the navy and everything it represented. I loved to fly. But I also loved to speak, to share, to convince, and to teach people.

One thing that helped me find my real purpose in life was starting graduate work in behavioral psychology. I took night courses for a master's degree program in semantics and propaganda. My master's work featured a fascinating, in-depth study of Communist interrogation methods during the Korean War. When they captured one of our men, they used a series of simple questions to discover whether he was the purposeful leader type or the purposeless follower. These questions included the following: Where are you from? Do you have a girl back home? What are you going to do when you get back? What kind of job do you want? What is your favorite baseball team? What is your favorite football team?

Mixed in with the somewhat innocuous inquiries were other questions: What are you fighting for? What does freedom mean to you? What are your religious beliefs? These, of course, were the key questions in the interrogation. The Communists knew that a man without commitment to a source higher than himself could be much more easily persuaded with human logic. In other words, if he didn't have a strong faith, he could be swayed with a chunk of beef in his soup, a carton of cigarettes, or a letter from his mother.

When a prisoner answered the questions vaguely and with non-specific shrugs, the Communists knew they had a candidate for one of their minimum security camps where prisoners could be indoctrinated, converted, and brainwashed. They knew from experience, and their statistics proved, that a man who doesn't stand for something will fall for anything.

On the other hand, the prisoners who answered questions specifically, who seemed to understand what freedom was about, and who seemed to have purposes and goals mixed with strong religious beliefs were put into the heavily guarded camps. Those men faced barbed wire, attack dogs, machine guns, constant interrogation, beatings, starvation, and torture.

The most fascinating aspect of these studies showed that according to statistics provided by the Communists themselves, the death and disease rate in the maximum security camps was much lower than that in the minimum security camps. In minimum security, individuals were there for the duration. They had good food, blankets, a warm place to sleep and, most important, comfortable libraries filled with plenty of indoctrination material. Ironically enough, in that country club atmosphere, many of the prisoners died rather quickly and easily.

But the men with purpose who went to the maximum security camps and suffered starvation and beatings actually fared better. Amazingly, their overall health was better. Many of them never stopped trying to escape. And many of them did. What kept them going was their purpose. They had something to live for, and they never gave up.

I WANTED CAKE A LA MODE EVERY DAY

My graduate studies caused me to be even more ambivalent about my situation. What was *my* real purpose? Flying was terrific, but probing the frontiers of the human mind was even more intriguing. I tried to figure out what kind of job I *really* wanted. Just exactly what was I doing in the U.S. Navy?

It's quite obvious to me now that I wanted my cake a la mode and I wanted it every day. But that was not to be. I had to choose: settle into the navy's straight-ahead, regimented system where I could rise slowly through the ranks but never be able to fly anything but a desk, or move out into civilian life where I would have more freedom to develop my potential, my natural gifts—where I could set my own goals and reach them at my own speed.

My regrets were deep, but my image of what I could become was deeper and stronger. In 1961 I resigned from the navy to become a public relations consultant for private industry, and I later specialized in financial and shareholder PR work. For the next four years I mixed the vital skills I had learned in the navy—practicing self-discipline, stressing teamwork, setting goals, and hitting targets—with my natural gifts of speaking, teaching, and convincing others.

During that time I joined the Ampex Corporation and moved to Redwood City, California. One of my first assignments was to introduce the magic of videotape technology to the broadcasting industry. Ampex had invented the first videotape recorder, and part of my work involved attending various trade shows to demonstrate how things looked as real on videotape as they did in life.

---

*M*ost people spend their entire lives on
a fantasy island called "Someday I'll"

——————— ✳ ———————

At last it seemed that I was beginning to achieve my goal. I was writing, creating, and presenting my ideas to others. But I still had a problem. I wasn't in the exciting front line or on the cutting edge of public relations and behavioral psychology as I had envisioned I would be. I was in a technical environment, and a lot of the writing I did was for manuals that were factual, necessary, and very boring. I had crept forward a step or two, but it seemed that in some ways I was slipping back to the technical level I'd been concerned with as a midshipman and as a pilot.

JIMINY CRICKET HEADS FOR THE SALK INSTITUTE

In 1965 I decided to make another career change. An opportunity came to work as a consultant to the president of the Salk Institute for Biological Studies, which just happened to be located in La Jolla,

California, just a few miles from where I had grown up. My chief responsibility at the institute was to be fund raising, and I moved back to my hometown with high hopes and even higher enthusiasm.

The Salk Institute staff, headed by Jonas Salk himself, was on the cutting edge of biological research. Their studies centered on some of civilization's most pressing questions. How do cells reproduce and why? When you cut your finger and the cells grow back, how do they know when to stop? Why does cancer cause cells to go crazy and grow uncontrollably?

In short, the Salk Institute was discovering how the human system functions at a biological level. What an opportunity to be part of helping humankind while I was reaching my own goals as well!

By working for the Salk Institute, I could observe the connections and correlations between the biological side and the psychological side of human beings. Even as a young boy, I had wondered and marveled at how certain people could be so happy and contented, even though they didn't seem to have all the "necessary" things such as a fancy car, lots of money, attractive looks, or star status. What makes these people tick? What is the secret of their success? How much is biological, and how much is psychological? How much of happiness and contentment is inborn, and how much is learned?

It was what I had been after all my life. I was excited about the potential in every human being. I wanted to be someone who could help people understand the profound truth in a child's story like *The Little Engine That Could*. I wanted to be like Jiminy Cricket in Walt Disney's version of Pinocchio. I wanted to steer people away from the folly of going to Pleasure Island and wasting all of what they have and are on goal-less, purposeless living.

For years I had been struggling and searching. Just maybe, at the Salk Institute, it could be "all the way in one play." Maybe it would all come together, and I could get out of the dog-eat-dog world and fulfill my dreams and goals in a setting of medical and scientific research designed to make the world a better place.

I had no real experience in fund raising, but I thought I knew something about human behavior. So I jumped into my work with both feet, and at first it seemed that I succeeded only in putting my foot in my mouth. But one of my first real successes was arranging a large donation from a developer who had just built the largest condominium apartment building in La Jolla. At dinner on the occasion of his fortieth birthday, he offered the donation before I even had a chance to bring up the subject. "I'm sorry that we have a lot of our money tied up right now," he said. "All we can give the Salk Institute is $100,000."

My fork poised halfway to my mouth and then dropped into my peas. "Oh, that's all right," I managed in a broken falsetto as the waiter scooped up the pea debris. Taking a deep breath, I barely managed, "Could you drop by tomorrow and chat with our treasurer?" I think I was beginning to hyperventilate. It's difficult to talk and hold your breath at the same time.

"Yes," he said, "that will be fine."

The next day I called the Salk Institute treasurer to tell him about the "little contribution" we'd be getting just before lunch. He didn't believe me at first, but when I brought my new friend into his office, he got very excited.

As the donor handed over one of the largest individual contributions ever given the Salk Institute up to that time, our treasurer turned several different colors and blurted haltingly, "we . . . err . . . err . . . certainly appreciate this generous gift, Mr. Check."

"Mr. Check" and I chuckled as we left the treasurer staring at the beauty of a one followed by five zeros. The donor's real name was Bob Kelce, whose aversion for publicity made him as modest as he is generous. He and his lovely wife, Diane, became some of our closest friends, a very open and genuine family who never flaunted their financial status but always treated everyone the way they wanted to be treated. They have an inner quality that can't be purchased.

Private donors with $100,000 checks were not easy to come by, however, and I soon started using methods I had learned in my navy PR work with the entertainment world. To help the Salk Institute become better known on the East Coast, I helped arrange "An Evening With Peggy Lee" at the Waldorf Astoria in New York City, where we raised $50,000.

Next I helped the Women's Auxiliary of the Salk Institute organize a "1001 Arabian Nights Hole-in-One Golf Tournament" at the Whispering Palms Country Club not far from La Jolla. We set up Arab-style tents on the lush fairways amid the sand traps and added a beauty pageant for good measure.

"1001 Arabian Nights" was another success, but I soon heard that the scientists and other academic fellows associated with the Salk Institute were beginning to question my methods. They were happy with the money raised, but they were a bit puzzled. Why did people have to be entertained in order to want to support science and help humankind?

I sensed that even Dr. Salk himself, no stranger to publicity and celebrity status, began to question this fund-raising approach. His discovery of a polio vaccine in 1954 had thrust him into the public eye, and to this day, his is one of the five or ten most recognized names in the world. Dr. Salk was used to the news media. He knew about publicity and promotion, but nonetheless he was understandably a bit uncomfortable with events like "1001 Arabian Nights."

As we discussed my fund-raising methods, I tried to share with the institute president, Augustus Kinzel, what I called Waitley's Law of Fund Raising. Back in my public relations days with the U.S. Navy, I quickly learned that to sell something, I had to illustrate the benefits and specific results and make it sound appealing and exciting in the process. When given a choice between having fun and doing something responsible and socially redeeming, most people will choose having fun almost every time.

Over the years I had discovered that few people buy anything because of its own good or worth. We buy things or contribute to causes according to our perception of the immediate pleasure or satisfaction involved. "In other words," I explained, "we do not want something because it's good, but we call something good because we want it!"

I was thoroughly convinced that the institute couldn't ask for private financial sponsorship simply because humankind would benefit. Strangely enough, most things that are good for us are often things that don't seem to be any fun. We lack the foresight to take the long-range view and think of the long-lasting benefits, the extension of life and well-being that can come if we contribute to a cause like that of the Salk Institute. Most of us are much more sure of how we want to feel *right now*.

Try as I might, I could not get the majority of the institute's scientific staff to understand that we had to get people to finance a dream without getting too specific about just what the dream entailed. People prefer to feel than think. They respond rather quickly and easily to being entertained, but it takes a lot more effort to educate them or appeal to their noble intentions.

THE PROBLEM WITH "SOMEDAY I'LL . . ."

Now, of course, I speak to thousands of people each year who are somewhere on the corporate ladder, and I am constantly amazed at their lack of specific goals. Managing by objectives (MBO) has been around for years. Numerous books, audiocassettes, videos, and seminars emphasize goal setting. But even with all this input, many people still lack the specificity necessary to set suitable goals for themselves and reach them.

I have found that most people devote more time to planning a vacation than to planning their careers and lives. They want to be the best, but being the best remains an undiscovered treasure lying somewhere out there on "Someday I'll . . ." They don't even know where this imaginary island is located, but they talk about it as if it holds a lot of promise for them. "Someday I'll get that promotion." "Someday I'll change jobs and do what I'm really good at." "Someday I'll go back to school and get the college credits I need to move forward."

For countless unhappy, unsuccessful people out there, getting through the day is a primary ambition. They set no other daily goals. They float along like driftwood in a slow-moving river. They take whatever job they happen to find and exert the least amount of effort possible. They often go to work with an attitude that says, "Well, I'll see what's happening. The boss will be gone, and I won't have to work very hard." Or one that says, "I've done that so many times, I won't even have to *think* today and the time will go fast."

They focus on lunch breaks, coffee breaks, quitting time, and pay day. They are very religious and always spend Fridays thanking God for the coming weekend. On Mondays they ask the Lord for the strength to get through another week. But as Peggy Lee's ageless line asks, "Is that all there is?"

LIFE IS NOT A POPULARITY CONTEST

I have my own system of goal setting that I want to share with you in the next chapter. To show you how this system works, I will use as a case study my final and most ambitious fund-raising endeavor for the Salk Institute. Although he may not have been comfortable with my methods, Dr. Salk was gracious and generous. I came to treasure my few discussions with him, and in the four years I worked with the institute, Jonas Salk became an inspiration and role model. From him I learned that we must discover how the healthy organism functions before we can find what prevents a particular disease.

Dr. Salk doesn't even know that he was the one who inspired me to finish my graduate studies in behavioral psychology. I read his books and listened to his insights, presented to help all of us think about studying life, health, and successful behavior instead of concentrating on disease, unhealthy behavior, and causes for failure.

To this day, I count Jonas Salk as one of the most influential people to affect my life and thinking. In a recent article on human potential, he said:

> Ideas came to me as they do to all of us. The difference is I took them seriously. I didn't get discouraged that others didn't see what I saw. I had trust and confidence in my perceptions, rather than listening to dogma and what other people thought. I didn't allow anyone to discourage me—and everyone did. But life is not a popularity contest. [1]

I especially like those words because they counter beautifully the myriad of myths that bombard us today with advice to do what is tension relieving rather than what is goal achieving.

Over twenty years ago, I took a "graduate course" in purpose and goal setting. Undaunted by the scientific staff's doubts about my fundraising methods at the Salk Institute, I organized what today is known as the Andy Williams Shearson-Lehman Brothers Open, one of the leading events on the PGA golfing tour. The story of how this tournament emerged from what looked like a hopeless maze of difficulties and frustrations is in the next chapter.

✳

OPPORTUNITIES MISSED
(or The Curse of Permanent Potential)

There was a very cautious man
Who never laughed or played
He never risked, he never tried
He never sang or prayed
And when he one day passed away
His insurance was denied
For since he never really lived
They claimed he never died.

—paraphrase of a verse by an unknown author

CHAPTER 7

THE RATCHET EFFECT: TWO CLICKS FORWARD, ONE BACK

AFTER EXPERIENCING SOME success in raising funds for the Salk Institute with Peggy Lee and "1001 Arabian Nights," I began to plan bigger and better events. An idea for what became the pièce de résistance came while I was playing golf with the late Frank Rhoades, the "Walter Winchell" of San Diego whose well-read column ran regularly in the *San Diego Union*.

It was February 1966, and the Bob Hope Desert Classic in Palm Springs and the Crosby Pro-Am at Pebble Beach were in the news. Frank and I began asking each other: "If San Diego, with sixty-five golf courses, is known as 'Golf Land USA,' why can't we hold a big-time celebrity tournament, too?"

The idea intrigued us, and we brainstormed possibilities. Because neither of us was a very good golfer, we had a great deal of time to talk as we wandered the rough of Whispering Palms Golf Course searching for our hazard-seeking golf balls.

Our brainstorm session was informal, but we followed a basic rule: we thought of every possibility we could and didn't shoot down any of them in the first go-around. One of the mistakes that many people make while brainstorming is to evaluate and judge ideas as they are given. For successful brainstorming, never shoot yourself down when you are coming up with ideas, or you will never get off the ground. Nothing ever gets attempted if all objectives must first be overcome.

We knew San Diego had the weather, the population, and the transportation arteries necessary for a major tournament. In fact, a modest PGA tournament called the San Diego Open had been going on for some years. Our brainstorming zeroed in on big names we could tie into our celebrity pro-am idea. We needed celebrities who were associated with playing golf or with philanthropy. We came up with Perry Como, Danny Kaye, Frank Sinatra, and Andy Williams.

We also brainstormed the recipient of benefits from the tournament. Frank was partial to the USO because San Diego was a strong navy town. Naturally, I thought of the Salk Institute and Jonas Salk's national and international reputation.

After we had all our ideas in place, we went back over them to decide which ones would really work. As we went through the celebrity names, we observed that Danny Kaye was involved with UNICEF at the time and probably would not be available. Frank Sinatra was already associated with another big golf event. Perry Como was a good possibility because I already had connections with him from my days of navy PR work. But Perry lived on the East Coast, and getting him involved with a West Coast event might be difficult.

We settled on Andy Williams because he was young, on the upswing in popularity, and located in the West. He also liked playing in celebrity golf tournaments and had a reputation for being a truly nice guy.

There it was. On the Whispering Palms Golf Course, somewhere near the fifteenth tee, in February 1966, I decided on my goal: to develop and produce the Andy Williams Open in San Diego as a major PGA tour event, with a celebrity pro-am that would benefit the Salk Institute.

I pictured myself in my new role. I envisioned the moment when I would be standing on the eighteenth green at the awards ceremony, watching as the winning check was handed to the pro with the best score. I also pictured another check—the one for $100,000 or $200,000 or perhaps $500,000 that would be given to the Salk Institute because of the money raised for a worthy cause through the celebrity pro-am part of the tournament.

The more I thought of my goal, the more it started to become an obsession. I'm not quite sure if Frank and I ever did finish that round of golf. We may have picked up and left. I was too busy making plans for my new venture to remember.

ANY OLD ROAD CAN TAKE YOU TO NOWHERE

Of course, I had no idea how my new goal would literally change my life. It would take months, even years, before the Andy Williams Open would be a reality. Organizing that tournament and making it happen was a graduate course in goal setting for me. I had always been goal oriented, but I would gain a new level of understanding and appreciation for establishing well-defined goals.

Setting a goal starts with a dream, a desire for something you really want. Planning is the road map that leads you to your destination. Motivation is the fuel that takes you there. But first you have to have a goal. If you don't know where you're going, any road will take you there, and it really won't matter what you try to do with your life. If you don't clearly know where you're going in life, how will you know when you get there?

But such aimless living is like traveling on a ship without a rudder. Ask any crew what it's like to sail a rudderless ship, and they'll tell you it's frustrating to go in circles. Purposeless, rudderless living leads to the frustration of negative attitudes and poor self-esteem.

BE SPECIFIC IN DEFINING YOUR GOALS

The secret to productive living is to establish clearly defined goals, write them down, and focus on them several times a day with words, pictures, and emotions. Think about your goals *as if you have already achieved them.* To clearly define your goals, you must be specific. People often talk about achieving happiness, wealth, or success, but these ever-popular attractions are not goals. They are not even purposes. Happiness, wealth, and success are by-products of having a purpose in life and setting specific goals to carry out that purpose.

In the seminars I lead, each person takes a sheet of paper and writes down what would give the most fulfillment in both life and work. Any number of items can be listed, but each one must be specific. The more defined the item, the better the aim and focus.

For example, I might write the following:

• I want to be happy. (Under that I write down a list of the conditions and achievements that will make me happy.)

- I want to make money. (Under that I write down how much money I want to make and when. I list the services I will provide to earn that money.)

- I want to be famous. (By excelling in what?)

- I want to be president of the company. (By taking what career steps over what period of time, with what new knowledge and skill developments?)

- I want to own my own business. (Where, when, and in what industry or field? What are the growth trends, capital requirements, and start-up considerations?)

- I want to spend more time with my friends and family. (I do? Then I list my current activities and eliminate the ones I can do without or postpone. I put down the trade-offs and the options.)

To make this easier to understand, I'll explain it as if you were a seminar participant who completed the exercise. You would soon see that without specific goals, you are engaging in wishful thinking. Specific goals should reflect personal wants and needs, not what others want from you. As you study your list, think about how much each item means to you. Try to clearly imagine achieving each goal. Consider the consequences of each goal, if any, and how reaching that goal will have an impact on your life and the lives of others involved. Ask yourself, Which goals come closest to really fulfilling my personal definition of success—being the best I can be?

At this point, you may feel like erasing some goals and adding others. Take another sheet of paper, and revise the first list of goals in a new order of priority. Number each goal, and try to have no more than ten. Take time to evaluate the order of importance you have given the goals. As you concentrate on all ten goals, you may find the list should be rearranged. Ultimately, you will come to recognize the goals that mean the most to you.

After you have prioritized your goals from one to ten, underline the top three. Rewrite these goals on a three-by-five card, or pencil them into a monthly planner. Carry these primary goals with you everywhere and refer to them often. When faced with any decision about how to spend your time, ask yourself if your choice will help you or hinder you in achieving your paramount goals in life at the moment.

HOW MY ANDY WILLIAMS DREAM BECAME REALITY

Let's go back to February 1966 and that first glow of enthusiasm for what was then simply a dream—the Andy Williams Open. In those days my goal-setting techniques were basic and crude. I had a lot to learn, and bringing my dream to reality would be a stern teacher.

Perhaps the most valuable lesson I would learn was how to use what I came to call the ratchet effect—cranking forward a few notches toward the goal, slipping back or seeming to stand still, and then cranking forward again. The ratchet effect is the only way I know to break down a major goal into bite-size, achievable chunks and move ahead with specific progress. The challenge is to set the target just out of reach, but not out of sight.

I was to learn that the bigger the idea, the longer it usually takes to bring it to fruition. Any number of indifferent or obstacle-creating people may want to squelch your idea and frustrate your goals. Always be prepared to sell your idea to people who don't believe you can do it and who may not even think that it should be done. The world may think there is not room for your goal. Others may consider your goal impractical, harmful, or stupid.

The minute you see truths in a dream or a goal you have, the world will come along with its myths and its reasons why it just won't work. You may hear some comments like these: "It's never been done before." "It's already been done very well." "It will cost too much." "You are bucking tradition (or procedure, or the system) . . . that just isn't how we do things around here."

With opposition coming from all sides, it's no wonder many people opt for purposeless, stress-free living. After all, who needs the hassle? But I like what the Reverend Robert H. Schuller told his son, Bob, after the younger Schuller had struggled through four long, hard years to get a college degree: "The tassel is worth the hassle."

The "tassel" I was after was getting Andy Williams to agree to be a part of my new golf tournament and then having that tournament actually happen. As I came home from that life-changing round of golf with Frank Rhoades, I realized that Andy still didn't know about our plans. We had a goal, but it wasn't Andy's goal—yet.

So I outlined the entire goal and plan on paper until I was completely comfortable with all the details. As I discovered later, there were plenty of holes in my plan, but at that point I felt I was ready. I took a deep breath and dialed NBC. Using techniques I had learned in previous PR work, I gave my own name first and tried to speak with authority: "This is Denis Waitley calling for Andy Williams."

And what, his secretary asked, did I want to speak to Andy Williams about?

"The Andy Williams Open, which will bring big-time golf to San Diego, California," I said matter-of-factly, as if the tournament was already a reality.

Somehow it worked. Andy came to the phone and was polite but only mildly interested. He sensed immediately that I was young and inexperienced and didn't have many of the real answers I needed. "Fine, sounds good," he said. "If you ever get it off the ground, let me know."

But that's all the encouragement I needed. It was full steam ahead at thirty-one knots. I took a trip to the NBC studios and somehow talked my way backstage for half an hour with Andy. There I learned that he was an admirer of Jonas Salk and that if one wanted to do a pro-am tournament with celebrities, one contacted Maurie Luxford who knew more about putting together celebrity tournaments than anyone in the country. Luxford was one of the brains behind the Bing Crosby Pro-Am at Pebble Beach. In Andy's opinion, he was the man I should see next.

OUTSIDE OF NOTHING, WHAT CAN I DO FOR YOU?

I called Maurie Luxford and got one of the strongest negative reactions of my life. He let me know that it had taken twenty years to build the Bing Crosby event, and you "don't add another celebrity tournament just like that." He also added phrases like these: "You'll never be able to do it . . . the world doesn't need another celebrity tournament . . . the public doesn't want one . . . the PGA doesn't want one . . . you're not experienced enough . . . you can't do it . . . you shouldn't do it . . . it doesn't make any sense . . . outside of that, what can I do for you?"

But I refused to back off. When Luxford saw that I wasn't going to give up that easily, he suggested that I go up to the March Field Air Force Base where a pro-am event was soon to be held. By seeing all the work involved in a little celebrity tournament, I would better understand what I was up against.

Ratcheting forward one big notch, I went to March Field where I introduced myself to Maurie Luxford. After talking with me, he took me over to chat with Andy Williams who also happened to be there as part of the celebrity festivities.

Andy was polite but asked, "What was your name again?" Along with my name I gave him another verbal outline for the proposed Andy Williams Open in San Diego. They both listened but seemed noncommittal.

But somehow, what I said must have gotten through to Maurie Luxford. Three days later he called to tell me he had told Andy Williams he would try to help me with my project!

My ratchet cranked ahead at least three notches at that point. But during the next few months it slipped a few cogs as I started getting flak and protests from all sides. Andy Williams flatly insisted that the Professional Golfers' Association be involved in any tournament with his name on it. But Maurie Luxford didn't want the PGA involved. And when I talked with PGA officials, I found them extremely cool toward the idea of another celebrity tournament.

It seems that golf pros aren't really fond of pro-am celebrity events. When they do play in one, they are kind, gracious, and smile a lot, but secretly they grit their teeth as they are matched up with amateurs who have handicaps of eighteen and the ability to spray tee shots into ponds, crowds, and even fellow players.

To add to my concerns, I heard that other big names were planning pro-am events of their own. Frank Sinatra was thinking of doing another one. Dean Martin and Jackie Gleason were also talking it up. It seemed that all of a sudden people really weren't top show business personalities if they weren't thinking about sponsoring a golf tournament.

Meanwhile, back at the Salk Institute, the news of my efforts caused the standard reaction: just how do science and celebrity golf mix? I began to feel about as small as I did that day when Admiral Lee told Admiral Burke I wanted to be a PR man. Maybe I would have been better off to have stayed in the navy flying a desk.

WHAT'S IN THIS FOR YOU, WAITLEY?

The turning point came, however, when I attended a Tournament of Stars at the Peacock Gap Country Club in San Rafael, California. Andy Williams was to be there, and when he alighted from his helicopter at the driving range, I was there, waiting to greet him. I had a problem. Would Andy recognize me or remember my name?

Not to worry! I purchased a huge bucket of driving range golf balls and used them as my "ticket" to get past the white lines and the marshals who were trying to keep the crowds from mobbing the celebrities. "Where are you going?" one of the marshals asked me as I went across the line.

"I have this bucket of balls for Andy Williams, and I'm taking them to him down at the driving range," I replied.

He let me by, and as I put the bucket of balls down in front of Andy, I said, "Hello, Mr. Williams, you may or may not remember me, but I am Denis Waitley, the consultant who wants you to sponsor the Andy Williams Open to benefit the Salk Institute."

"Oh, yes," Andy replied as he teed up. "I didn't recognize you, but maybe we ought to talk about that sometime."

If you don't know where you're going, it doesn't matter if your alarm doesn't go off

---

✱

By this time one of the other marshals realized I was an intruder, and he quickly escorted me back across the lines. I followed Andy around the course for a while, but I realized there would be no way to talk to him further unless I could somehow get him alone. Why not try the locker room? He had to go there after his round of golf to change clothes.

When Andy came into the clubhouse, there I was, sitting on the bench waiting for him. I realized he might not give me much more time than it would take to remove his golf shoes, so I didn't waste a second. I said, "Look, I realize I'm making a pest of myself, but I really believe this tournament is doable, and you're the one to do it."

Andy looked me right in the eye and said, "I have just one question that I'm going to ask you before I give you my answer. If I lend my name to this tournament to benefit the Salk Institute, and you're able to do the things that you are talking about, what's in it for you? Do you benefit financially? Do you become the honcho of the whole thing? What's the bottom line? Where do you really fit in?"

I stared right back and told him the truth, "I'm a consultant to the president of the Salk Institute, and this is simply part of my job. I'm dedicated to promoting and financing the research of the institute. I don't want any glory. I don't want a job with you. I don't want compensation from you or any cut from tournament proceeds. I'm getting my salary from the institute, and that's all I expect to get."

Andy Williams smiled, "That's the answer I've been waiting for— that you're doing this to help the Salk Institute and not doing it for yourself. Why don't you fly back with us to Los Angeles, and we'll talk some more."

Several more cranks on the ratchet for Waitley. I got in a private jet with Andy Williams and other passengers who included Dan Rowan and Dick Martin from "Laugh-In," several golf pros, and Ed Crowley, vice president of the Bob Hope Desert Classic.

As Andy and I talked during the flight, I sketched some of my public relations background and mentioned Peggy Lee and Perry Como, names I hoped would convince him that I hadn't just fallen off the turnip truck. Andy agreed to lend his name to my golf tournament idea, but he remained firm in his request that the PGA be involved and the Andy Williams Open be a part of the official tour. It had to be a major event, just like the Crosby and Hope tournaments.

"Talk with my PR man, Charlie Pomerantz, and see what you can come up with," Andy said as we parted.

ANDY AND DR. SALK HIT IT OFF

Charlie Pomerantz proved to be a valuable ally. With his help I got a bargain rate to rent a Lear jet and fly Andy Williams into San Diego for a visit and a personal look at where we might play the tournament. I also arranged to have him meet Dr. Salk and tour the institute. Andy stayed at the La Costa Country Club resort, which just happened to be a stone's throw from the institute.

Andy and Dr. Salk hit it off beautifully at dinner. Both very modest and caring individuals, they never let their egos get in each other's way as they discussed how they could somehow merge science with a show business sporting event and still remain dignified, all with the goal of benefiting the Salk Institute and humankind.

After dinner, Dr. Salk took Andy to the institute for a special after-hours tour. Andy was so impressed with the institute's work and the sincerity and modesty of Dr. Salk that on the spot he decided to donate the first $50,000 in proceeds from his newest album, *Born Free*.

My goal-achieving ratchet was clicking now. Merv Adelson (who today is chief executive officer of Lorimar Productions) was one of the key developers and owners of the La Costa resort at that time. He put me in touch with one of the most powerful men in the Professional Golfers' Association, Jack Tuthill, the tournament director. Tuthill was the one to see about tournament dates, and he could tell me how such tournaments are actually played.

A championship course, La Costa had already hosted other major PGA events, and Merv Adelson was quite willing to make the course available for the new tournament if we could work things out. With its magnificent club facilities and demanding golf holes, La Costa was a perfect site for the Andy Williams Open.

With high hopes I flew to Florida for an audience with Jack Tuthill and the executive director of the PGA, Bob Creasey. It turned out that Tuthill was a busy man, and I literally had to catch him on a golf course and talk to him as we walked the fairways. He was lukewarm to my idea, citing problems with scheduling in an already crowded PGA schedule for that year. I was hoping for a fall date, but there just weren't that many openings. About the only dates he could give me for a one-day or two-day pro-am, followed by a regular four-day tournament, landed on Thanksgiving weekend.

I made a proposal in writing to the PGA and sought the Thanksgiving dates for the Andy Williams Open. A few weeks later I received approval to hold the tournament over Thanksgiving weekend, 1967.

Ecstatic, I called Andy Williams and gave him the news.

"I'm sorry. Thanksgiving just won't work," he said. "Nobody will watch, and nobody will want to play. Thanksgiving is meant for families. I always spend Thanksgiving with my family, and I think most people feel the same way. There is no way we could succeed with a Thanksgiving date."

I SEEMED TO SLIP BACK TO NOTCH ONE

My goal-seeking ratchet seemed to slip all the way back to notch one. As I watched the 1967 New Year's Day bowl games, I didn't even notice who was playing. I was a year into trying to reach my goal, but I seemed to be at a dead end. I didn't realize it at the time, but I was struggling with a major problem with goal setting. I had to recognize that if I was interested in doing something significant, I would have to allot enough time to accomplish my goal. For something as involved as organizing a national PGA event, two to three years probably wasn't that unreasonable.

As the final gun sounded for the last New Year's Day bowl game, I got my ratchet back in gear. Since I was stuck on a date for my Andy Williams Open, I thought about trying to merge our proposed event with the San Diego Open, which already existed. If the idea worked, we could wind up with a major tournament worth well over $100,000.

Early in January, I got together with officials from the Century Club, sponsors of the San Diego Open, and enthusiastically shared my plans. I pointed out all the advantages: national TV exposure, funds raised for the Salk Institute, greater prestige for San Diego, and fame and more respect for executives of the Century Club itself.

Although I like to say that a smile is the light of enthusiasm in a person's window, I have to admit that after my impassioned speech, all their lights went out. There was nary a smile in the room. Who was I to come in and tell them how to run their tournament? I heard all the reasons why it couldn't possibly work. Underneath it all, I detected a note of jealousy and fear.

Fortunately, I found a few goal miners in the organization, particularly Steve Horrell, a younger member of the Century Club. He said, "Look, this might work. Let's at least pursue it. We don't have to say yes, but let's not say no."

Steve Horrell was the key. The owner-manager of Singing Hills Country Club in San Diego, he eventually accepted the appointment of tournament chairman. Steve thought I had infectious enthusiasm, and he matched it with some of his own, plus a lot of solid business management skills.

Things moved fast in January 1967. By January 25, Steve Horrell had worked miracles, and everything somehow fell into place. The Century Club was willing to merge the San Diego Open with the Andy Williams pro-am celebrity event. Because of herculean efforts by Assistant City Manager Julian Wise, the city of San Diego was willing to get into the action by donating $50,000, as long as we used the Torrey Pines Municipal Golf Course as the site. Through Andy Williams, NBC came up with $125,000 for television rights.

I knew I could print a celebrity program with advertising sponsored by major golf equipment manufacturers and other firms that would be interested. With parking and admissions, we would have no trouble coming up with a purse of $165,000, which would turn out to be the third-largest purse on the PGA tour at that time.

My prior conversations with Merv Adelson and the La Costa Country Club gave me concern. I was committed to using the Torrey Pines Golf Course rather than La Costa. Fortunately, the two courses weren't that far apart, and we were able to arrange to use La Costa's much finer facilities, clubhouse, hotel, and restaurants as the entertainment headquarters. We even decided to play some of the pro-am rounds at La Costa while the major four-day professional tournament would be held at Torrey Pines.

WHEN THE GOING GETS TOUGH, THE TOUGH EAT CROW

My goal-seeking ratchet clicked beautifully in January 1967, but it sputtered and came to a grinding halt in February. On February 1 the PGA told me the entire package was acceptable, but the association couldn't see any firm dates for holding the tournament sometime early in 1968. Then just a week or so later, the PGA reneged completely, saying that the Andy Williams format was too similar to the Crosby and Hope tournaments being held at that same time of year. The officials wanted us to go back to the original Thanksgiving date they had given us earlier!

By now I had decided I would never eat turkey again. It looked as if I would have to eat crow. Not only did we have an unacceptable date, but quite possibly I had lost the Century Club its regular January date for the old San Diego Open!

People started telling me they wished they had never met me. There were many moments when I wished I'd never met them or ever played that round of golf with Frank Rhoades at Whispering Palms. But I decided to hang in there and believe some of my own philosophy. Once I started putting the dream together, I had to stay committed.

I flew back to Florida to talk once more with Bob Creasey. We agreed that Thanksgiving wouldn't work and that the final format would be a two-day pro-am followed by a four-day professional tournament among the pros only. Creasey said he would get back to me, and I waited until March 13 for his news that the PGA had approved the tournament and the six-day format but the dates were still not set.

A major reason for not setting any dates was the atmosphere of uncertainty that surrounded the PGA at that time. A large group of golf professionals apparently were threatening to secede from the PGA and arrange a new schedule of their own. In July of 1967, Steve Horrell and I, along with others on our local committee, went to Denver where the PGA was holding a championship tournament and some important business meetings. We were armed with our new suggestion for a tournament date, February 6–11, 1968.

OUR OPEN IS ALMOST CLOSED BY HOPI WARRIORS

We faced a major hurdle. Would-be sponsors of several other new tournaments were also in Denver, and all of us descended on the Brown Palace Hotel, site of the business meetings, to plead for a spot on the PGA schedule.

I saw Dean Martin's entourage there, and I began to wonder if we would even get a chance to plead our case. Andy Williams wasn't with us, and to the PGA officials, we were those "What were their names again?" people from San Diego. But somehow our lucky star landed in the right place—at the same negotiating table with the PGA officials we were trying to convince. One of them finally said, "Why don't we just give these San Diego people their dates?"

Just as I was getting ready to let out a whoop of joy, other whoops arose from the hotel lobby and soon turned into a warlike din. It literally sounded like a tribe of wild Indians had attacked the hotel. We all ran out onto the balcony above the lobby, and there they were—a large group of Hopi Indians in full headdress performing a ceremonial dance right in front of the registration desk. I never did figure out if it was a hotel publicity stunt or a bona fide protest movement by the Hopis. Whatever its intention, the war dance broke up the PGA meetings, and our discussion about the dates for the Open was never finished.

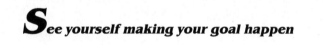

See yourself making your goal happen

✱

After we got back home from Denver, we learned that the PGA had more second thoughts about our tournament and the February dates we had suggested. Would we be interested in doing it on the same weekend as the NFL Pro Bowl football game in January? The PGA felt there was a real vacuum in the schedule between the Bob Hope Desert Classic and the Crosby Pro-Am at Pebble Beach. Perhaps our Andy Williams Open could fill that spot nicely. Were we interested?

There was only one small hitch. Holding the tournament on the Pro Bowl weekend meant no TV coverage. We turned it down. Without TV, Andy Williams wasn't interested, and without Andy Williams, we had nothing.

The PGA officials told me they would try to find another tournament to fill the Pro Bowl date in January, and I thought, *That's it—this is their nice way of saying "no deal."* I started making plans to leave the country on an extended five-year vacation, but a few days later I got another phone call at home around ten at night. It was Jack Tuthill of the PGA. Feeling a bit like the world's largest yo-yo, I said, "Yes, Jack, and what did I do now?"

"Your February dates are approved after all," Jack said. "We got another tournament to fill the January dates. You are on for February 6–11, 1968."

I called Andy Williams with the news. He said, "Are you sure?"

"As sure as I can be with the PGA," I said. "The Man told me so himself."

"Well, after you've gone to all this trouble, I guess we'll have to go through with it," Andy said with a little teasing in his voice.

"We've come this far," I joined in. "Why not?"

SOMEHOW THE RATCHET CLICKED ALL THE WAY

And go through with it we did. Somehow it all happened. That golf game with Frank Rhoades in February 1966 set off a ratcheting effect that materialized just two years later into the Andy Williams Open, with added celebrity pro-am fund raiser, held at the Torrey Pines Municipal Golf Course on February 6–11, 1968.

Those two years of struggle are a microcosm of what I try to teach today in my seminars. To accomplish any goal, you need a dream. You need to see yourself making it happen. But it has to go beyond the idea and the vision. You have to do your homework. You have to put your goal in writing, plan your steps, and take them one at a time.

When the disappointments and defeats stop you momentarily, you must persist. Get help from people with proven track records. Be flexible, be willing to come at it from a different angle, if necessary, and never, never give up.

How sweet it was to sit in the booth on the eighteenth green that day at Torrey Pines with Chris Schenkel, Andy Williams, and Dr. Jonas Salk and watch Tom Weiskopf sink an eagle to win first prize of $30,000. It was an even greater thrill to see the Salk Institute collect over $100,000 raised by the celebrity pro-am and a special "Andy Tonight" program held at the San Diego Civic Theatre during the tournament.

Patrons paid $250 each to attend "Andy Tonight" and enjoy seeing him perform as well as watching a parade of celebrities that seemed almost endless: Bob Hope, Peggy Lee, Henry Mancini, the Osmond Brothers, the Lennon Sisters, Joey Bishop, Bob Newhart, Rowan and Martin, Dean Martin, Jack Nicklaus, Fred MacMurray, Lee Trevino, Jack Benny, Phil Harris, and on and on into the night as the searchlights shone over the admiring crowd.

Today the tournament is known as the Andy Williams Shearson-Lehman Brothers Open. The celebrity pro-am is still a major feature, and though the Salk Institute no longer benefits, many other San Diego nonprofit organizations do. In February 1987 Susan and I attended a twentieth anniversary party for the tournament and enjoyed a reunion with people like Andy Williams, Pat Boone, and Ed Crowley. Although Andy and I hadn't seen each other in nearly twenty years, he still recalled that day in the clubhouse when he asked me, "What's in it for you?" and I told him, "Nothing, it's part of my job." That bit of integrity stuck in his mind after twenty years—and come to think of it, it sticks in mine.

I LEFT SALK INSTITUTE WITH MIXED EMOTIONS

I stayed with the Salk Institute through 1968, but early in 1969 I left to pursue a career as head of my own consulting firm and to complete requirements for a doctorate in human behavior. I treasure the four years I spent there and will always remember my few personal encounters with Dr. Jonas Salk as some of the high points of my life. What I learned from reading his books, listening to him, and observing him was priceless. As I watched him in the laboratory and saw how he handled himself and pursued his goals, I developed my own convictions about the need for high purpose and always learning more.

You may not ever work out the details for an event like a PGA golf tournament, or you may do something far more important and significant. But the principles for finding a purpose and setting and reaching meaningful goals remain the same, whether you're planning a sales presentation or a wedding shower for the daughter of a friend. You can be sure of one thing. Sooner or later you will need to understand and use the ratchet effect.

We are not all cut out to be straight *A* students, celebrities, world-class athletes, or CEO's of major companies. We are designed, however, to make the most of the abilities, talents, skills, and intelligence we possess. We are designed to be the best we can be. The happiest people in the world are those who are doing something they feel is worth their effort and who are working up to their potential. Perhaps the most splendid achievement of all is the continuing quest to surpass ourselves.

Setting goals is only part of that quest. I have spent the last two chapters talking about having a meaningful purpose in life and fulfilling that purpose with specific goals. Setting goals is important but learning how to move out and get things done deserves special attention. We'll look at that in chapter 8.

*I*F IT'S TO BE, IT'S UP TO ME!

BILLED AS ONE of the greatest college football games of all time, a recent Fiesta Bowl matched Penn State and Miami for the mythical national title on network television. Penn State eked out a 14–10 victory that included a nail-biting goal-line stand in the closing minutes. Somehow, Penn State's stubborn defense held off Miami's talented Heisman Trophy-winning quarterback, Vinny Testaverde, one last time and thwarted the Hurricanes' final frenzied effort to pull out a victory.

In the hectic jubilation following the final gun, TV cameras zeroed in on various players, including one of Penn State's All-American linebackers who assessed the game with words to this effect: "It was our defensive backs who really did it. Their receivers just didn't want to catch the ball. They heard footsteps all night long, and they just didn't want to get hit."

✳ ✳ ✳

Miami's players, particularly Testaverde's receivers, might offer a different opinion, but the records show that they did not have a very productive evening. Again and again, Testaverde was intercepted as he marched toward the Penn State goal line. Miami's players had their game plan, they had their goal—to be the best football team in the land—but they didn't get it done. On that fateful January day, Penn State was just a few points and a few plays better and emerged the mythical national champion.

From football and other sports, we can derive helpful analogies that give us some clues as to why people may set goals but not reach them. Everything may seem to be in place, but they still fail to make it happen. Why?

Perhaps they "hear the footsteps" of something or someone they fear will make them drop the ball.

Perhaps the stress and the pressure are just too much, and they choke.

Or they may develop "loser's limp," a ploy sometimes sub-consciously used by a ballplayer who drops the winning pass in the end zone or blows the winning lay-up at the buzzer. He pulls up lame, and the crowd has to understand that he didn't make the winning play because he "hurt himself." When people have all kinds of excuses ready for why they still haven't gotten off the ground or why they fail to close the deal, maybe they, too, are afflicted with loser's limp.

And then there are times when people get in over their heads. They talk a better game than they can really play.

WHY SOME PEOPLE JUST DON'T GET MUCH DONE

In my studies of human behavior I have come across three basic personality types who display such behavior while seldom getting very much done. They are the victims, the sustainers, and the dreamers.

Victims are preoccupied with the past and concerned about things that cannot be controlled. They develop loser's limp, and their con-versations are peppered with the phrases "should have," "could have," "might have" and, of course, the well-known "if only."

Victims feel helpless. They tend to fix the blame on others. They see themselves as thermometers controlled by external circumstances rather than as thermostats that can control their destiny.

The victim mentality permeates society today. Millions of people actually believe they fail to reach their goals because they were in the wrong place at the wrong time. Or perhaps their horoscope just wasn't right that day. Their excuses roll out in a stream. The problem is the government or the deficit or the way the Japanese do business, or maybe they just know they are being persecuted because they belong to a certain group.

Victims often go back and blame their families. They may claim they had "the wrong parents." Even birth order has doomed them to failure and mediocrity. The firstborn's problems stem from having to spend all that time taking care of little brothers and sisters. The middle child just knows it all has to do with being caught between the firstborn and the baby in the family. The youngest blames it all on having to be the baby of the family and having to wear hand-me-downs.

Victims are ready believers of the myth we looked at earlier: "You can't fight City Hall." They just seem to continually have rotten luck. The most optimistic thought they can muster is, *Well, it could have been worse.*

Sustainers make very little progress toward future goals because they are too worried about the present. They want to keep things going smoothly, the way they always have been. By living only in the present, sustainers seldom plan for the future or learn from the past.

They love to say, "Why change what's working?" The basic problem is fear. Perhaps the pressure is getting too strong. They may think they hear footsteps, so why take any risks? They cover fears by acting as though they are moving forward, but everything they do is very safe and very predictable.

Sustainers are good at muddling through and "playing fire fighter." They go to the office to see if someone knows about a fire that needs to be put out. They rise to the present crisis, and fires fit that category perfectly.

Sustainers are survivors, and they are almost as plentiful in society as victims. The major goal is to make it through the week and enjoy the weekend. Obviously, the favorite myth is this: "Thank God it's Friday."

Dreamers talk a good game to explain their lack of accomplishments. Their dreams may inspire their imagination, but they never quite get into action. They never turn those dreams into goals, plans, and actual activities.

Dreamers live in a never-never land of make-believe, pipe dreams, and "Someday I'll. . . ." They are all ideas and no follow-through; all blow and no show.

Dreamers may think of a market-shattering concept or an engineering break-through in the shower, but they never get out of the shower, get dressed, and do anything about it. Dreamers have permanent potential. Their favorite myths start with "Someday I'll . . . " and "If only . . . ," but someday never comes.

TAKE ACTION TODAY, NOT TOMORROW

I've done my share of playing the victim, the sustainer, and the dreamer. Any of these behaviors is possible at certain times and in certain situations. All three of them have led millions down the path toward another major myth that cripples, impedes, and frustrates any goal-seeking individual:

WHATEVER WILL BE WILL BE

"Que Sera, Sera" was a charming love song in years past, but it makes a lousy philosophy for life.

When the tentacles of this myth and its cousins—victimitus, survivalism, and pipe dreaming—start to coil themselves about you, you need to act fast and whip out the countering truth that can get you moving again:

IF IT'S TO BE, IT'S UP TO ME!

Instead of believing that things are out of control and you're helpless, convince yourself that you are in control and the day belongs to you. When you write your own script, you go into a totally different kind of behavior that I like to call proactive, or Action TNT—Action Today, Not Tomorrow.

I see every day as belonging to me. Why? Because a loving God has given it to me to enjoy and use to its fullest. The road to failure is littered with missed opportunities. The road to success is paved with daily optimism. I realize that opportunity never knocks, because it resides within me. Opportunity means finding a way to think positively when everyone else around me is mired in negativism. It has been said, "Yesterday is a canceled check and tomorrow is an IOU. Only today can be traded in for hard cash." That's why every day is a fresh, new opportunity to cash in on the abundance life offers.

Why do individuals fall into the trap of thinking like victims, sustainers, or dreamers? Because it's, oh, so easy to become locked into present circumstances. People may be unhappy and want to reach in new directions, but they seem to be helpless. I've seen this attitude in people in all walks of life—office managers, factory workers, homemakers, and vice presidents. They don't see the potential opportunities around them as well as those within them, and they are paralyzed by fear of failure. They have let their almost limitless potential become saddled by limitations. They just can't look far enough or think big enough about where they can go or how they can fit in.

DON'T "TAKE CARE"—TAKE A RISK!

Another prevalent myth these days declares: "Why take a risk? Why stick your neck out? Nobody will care or notice anyway." If you have any sense of your inner worth, if you have any sense of self-respect, if you are even faintly aware of your tremendous potential and natural gifts, this kind of talk will fall on your deaf ears. You'll be much more interested in trying to succeed, even though the worst you might do is fail.

---

*L*ife is a do-it-with-God,
do-it-for-others,
do-it-to-yourself program

———————————— ✳ ————————————

The myths that squelch creative action are often disguised in quaint little sayings people use on one another every day. For example, has someone said to you this week as you parted company, "Take care" or "Be careful"? Obviously, no one is interested in recklessly trying to endanger life and limb. Perhaps "Take care" ought to be changed to "Go for it. You can handle it." How long has it been since you heard a friend say good-bye with the comment, "Don't work too hard"? Wouldn't it be better for that person to say, "Hit the home-run ball at work today"?

When individuals fear taking any kind of risk, they try to tell themselves they are happy living cautiously in the safety net of the old familiar routines. But, of course, they are not happy; they are lonely and bored, feeling inadequate and insecure. They aren't sure they know much about what it takes to succeed, but if they are sure of anything, it's how to avoid failure. This risk-free living is a myth complete in one word:

SECURITY

There is a lot of talk about security today. We are to make our financial future secure with savings plans, IRA's, and insurance. We are to make our homes secure with locks and burglar alarms. But you and I know that the probability of achieving total security is, indeed, a myth. The only totally secure person is one lying horizontally, lily in hand, six feet underground.

Beware when security becomes your major goal in life and your fulfillment and joy seem reduced to merely existing—sustaining the status quo. Actually, when you live this kind of careful life, you are still taking a heavy risk. You risk losing any prospects of real happiness, knowing the elation of reaching a meaningful goal and knowing deep down that you did the best you could and you are becoming the best you can be.

Life is inherently risky. Birth is a risk. Crossing the street is a risk. Life is full of risks, illness, accidents, terrorists, tax audits, layoffs, bankruptcy. But life is also filled with opportunities that can lead to joy—good health, love, a happy family, satisfying work, promotions, financial success, and self-fulfillment.

In her early forties, Dixie Oliver, the wife of a dear friend and colleague of mine, decided to get out of the house and take a risk. The home was operating efficiently, and the kids were nearly self-sufficient. She was, and still is, a good household manager and an outstanding mother. But something was on her mind.

Previously, she had been a teacher, but she had recently discovered and become excited about an educational concept called Montessori. She signed up for and devoted an entire year to graduate studies in Montessori education. Her commitment to her studies involved more than her spare time or a few hours a week; often she was busy from eight in the morning until ten or eleven at night, attending classes and doing homework.

Finally, she qualified for her graduate certificate and started her own Montessori school a few years ago. She used a church in downtown Atlanta as the site for her first class, which consisted of three small children. The venture wasn't an overnight financial bonanza. The majority of the early enrollees were on scholarships, which meant their families couldn't afford the tuition and needed financial assistance. But not to worry, that wasn't Dixie's major priority.

Dixie wanted to serve God by serving people. She wanted to help them prepare themselves to be the very best they could be. The money, to her, was not the driving force.

In only a few years she has built the school, by reputation, to an enrollment of over ninety students. She employs thirteen people, and the school generates a business base of over $100,000 per year. The important result of that decision Dixie made to take a risk, however, is that she has a positive, creative influence on the different families the school serves.

My friend asked Dixie not long ago, "If there were any place in the world you could be, doing anything you'd like to do, where would you be and what would you be doing?"

She smiled, with a glow in her eyes, and replied, "I'd be doing exactly what I'm doing right now!"

Dixie, like others who dare risking, failing, or succeeding, has countered the myth of security with the truth that reminds us,

THE REAL RISK IN LIFE IS DOING NOTHING

If you confine yourself to the boundaries of safe, familiar ground that is totally secure, you put overwhelming limitations on your opportunities for happiness. But when you break out of the old routines and shatter obstacles with a no-limitations approach to reaching goals, you open yourself up to all the bounties of life. If you refuse to take reasonable risks to gain your fair share of those bounties, you have no one to blame but yourself.

WHO IS YOUR SCAPEGOAT?

The Old Testament book of Leviticus describes the sacred custom of using a scapegoat once a year to atone for the sins, mistakes, and failures of the Israelite nation. In solemn ceremony, Aaron the high priest would lead a goat to the outskirts of the camp. There he would place his hands on the goat's head and confess over it all the sins of the Israelite people. Through this symbolic act, the goat took on the sins and was then allowed to "escape" and wander in the wilderness, presumably to die.

The term *scapegoat* is still with us today, but it is not used in reference to sacred ceremony. Now people use it to describe what they choose to blame for their problems or mistakes. Some people make scapegoats of their parents; others blame their woes on the government, the economy, the schools, their companies, their bosses—even their horoscopes!

Instead of working on what is going on inside them, they try to blame what is going on *around* them. It's always easier and more convenient to assume the answer or the blame lies elsewhere or with others. They write their own myth that says, "Life is a they'll-do-it-to-you-every-time existence. I'm a victim of forces I really can't resist."

But if I have learned anything in the past twenty years, it is that life is a do-it-to-myself program. And I always must accept personal responsibility for the quality of my performance. I am convinced that in the long run, rewards in life equal the quality of the service rendered.

The law of cause and effect is God's unfailing boomerang. What goes around always comes around. I have never told a lie that didn't haunt me or hurt me, and I have never done a good deed that didn't help me or heal me in some way.

You and I are not responsible for what happens "out there," for what others do or think. We are responsible only for how we choose to respond. We choose our attitude. The responsibility for you is yours. The responsibility for me is mine.

PROCRASTINATION IS A FAVORITE "HIDING PLACE"

When I am caught in opportunity-stifling behavior, such as scapegoating or trying to live risk-free, one of my favorite "hiding places" is procrastination. When I procrastinate, I never do today what I can put off until tomorrow—or maybe next week. Of course, I pay a heavy price. When I procrastinate, I have this gnawing feeling of being fatigued, always behind. I try to tell myself that I am actually taking it easy and gathering my energies for a new big push, but procrastination is another weaver of myths and lies. The truth is, procrastinating doesn't save me time or energy; it drains away both and leaves me with self-doubt and self-delusion.

At the very root of procrastination is fear. It may be a fear of failure, of not being able to succeed. Who doesn't want to put off failure until tomorrow? Besides, by tomorrow or next week or next month maybe something will change. Maybe that big break will materialize.

Often, perfectionists are great procrastinators. They cover themselves by stalling and delaying and waiting until the last minute and then tearing into a job with dust flying and complaints about "not enough time." The perfectionist-procrastinator is a master of using the excuse, "It was the best I could do on such short notice."

DON'T WIND UP "UNDER THE GUN"

We are all busy. Every day we seem to have a giant to-do list—people to see, projects to complete, letters to read and letters to write, calls to answer and calls to make, and then more calls to call back those who have called us and left a message. In his spiritual classic, *Making All Things New*, Henri Nouwen compares our lives to overstuffed suitcases that are bursting at the seams. We seem to always feel there is far too much to do, so we say, "I'm really under the gun this week."

Since learning the real story behind the phrase "under the gun," I have decided to quit using it to describe how I am living my life. I want to be more responsible, less the procrastinator, than the man who was the first to be under the gun.

According to my research, the story took place in the days of the magnificent sailing ships, probably the mid-1700s. The plot of this supposedly real-life drama centers on an anonymous young naval officer who reaps a reward for solving a problem and pays the consequences for creating the problem in the first place. We'll call him Ensign Noble and place him aboard the HMS *Intrepid* en route from England to the colonies.

It seems the colonists were engaged in a series of rebellions, and the Royal Navy was dispatched to deliver guns and munitions to the Crown's government in New England. Ensign Noble was given a special assignment that involved transporting a large cannon from Portsmouth, England, to Boston. The ensign's orders called for traveling with the cannon to ensure its safe passage and delivery to the proper authority.

After two days at sea, the *Intrepid* encountered heavy weather and was soon running before a northerly gale. Ensign Noble hastened to lash the huge cannon to the deck and get quickly below where he could find some dry clothes and a mug of hot soup. As he hurriedly secured the cannon, the ensign reasoned, "These ropes should hold it. It doesn't look like that much of a storm anyway."

Ensign Noble had been below only a few minutes when the storm suddenly increased in intensity. The cannon came loose and rumbled across the deck. Noble heard cries of warning from men on watch above and was horrified by the crashing sound of splintering wood. He leaped on deck just in time to see the great gun rolling out of control, heading back from the starboard rail to the port side, bearing down on two sailors who were frantically trying to work with some sails that had become fouled in the roaring winds.

Without a moment's hesitation, Ensign Noble threw himself in front of the mighty gun and somehow stopped it before it reached his two shipmates. Both his legs were broken under the tremendous weight of the cannon's wheels, but he saved the day by literally throwing himself under the gun.

The next morning Ensign Noble, on crutches and in much pain, arrived on the quarterdeck for a special ceremony in his honor. The entire crew assembled to watch the captain bestow on the young ensign his country's highest award for heroism. A great cheer went up as the captain pinned on the medal. But it soon fell to absolute silence as he finished his presentation by saying: "For placing his ship and shipmates in dire peril and being guilty of dereliction of his duty, Ensign Noble is sentenced to die before a firing squad, sentence to be carried out immediately."

The moral of the story is quite clear. Working hard, even heroically, to solve a problem is not to your credit if you created the problem in the first place.[1]

When most people use this phrase today, they usually refer to pressures and problems that they want to believe are not their own doing. But in more cases than they care to admit, they are under the gun because they have failed to take care of business.

HOW TO TELL IF YOU'RE A PROCRASTINATOR

Do you find yourself under the gun a bit too often? Perhaps you procrastinate more than you realize. Here are some suggestions that may reveal your tendencies in that direction.

1. Do I put off the tough jobs or avoid difficult assignments in the hope that things may change and I can get out of responsibility?

2. Do I put off important tasks by stalling with reorganizing my desk, cleaning my files, or sharpening my pencils?

3. Am I afraid of new situations, any kind of change or risk?

4. When I am faced with a difficult or unpleasant situation, do I have a tendency to get sick or even have accidents?

5. Have I ever delayed something or done something so badly that

someone else finally had to do it—which is exactly what I had in mind in the first place?

6. Do I avoid confronting others, even though I may have a valid complaint, a just cause, or some information that could really help the other person?

7. Do I tend to blame "them" or "it" for my failures or delay in reaching my goals?

8. Do I resort to criticism or sarcasm to get out of doing something difficult or tedious?

9. Do I put off physicals and dental checkups because I think I'm "too busy"?

10. Am I working at three-quarters or half speed in my job, and using the excuse that it's too boring?

11. Is my planner book full of goals that have not been met?

12. Do my to-do lists stay filled with many things that have yet to be done?

One of the best ways out of a prison of procrastination is to make the conscious decision to try *something*—to take even the smallest steps toward your goals. There are all kinds of ways to experiment and test new ground without risking the whole ball game on one play.

As I shared earlier, the only way to progress toward your goals is with the ratchet effect: good old trial and error, trial and error, and then—success! Not the mythical state of permanent success, but the exhilarating feeling of accomplishment that gets you ready to go on to the next goal and the next step toward more success.

WHY PROCRASTINATORS ARE AFRAID

Ironically enough, the major reasons people allow themselves to get under the gun are fear and lack of self-confidence. Quite simply, they procrastinate because they are afraid. Three major fears drive individuals to procrastination: (1) fear of the unknown; (2) fear of inferiority or looking foolish; and (3) fear of success.

We looked at fear of the unknown when we talked about being willing to take more risks. Tied closely to fear of the unknown can be fear of looking or feeling inferior. Procrastinators want to do their best, but they are afraid of not being able to cut it. They are often excellent critics, who can analyze exactly what's wrong with others. They can explain why sales are down, why the church is losing members, and so on. These people look at others who are trying to reach certain goals or do a particular job, and they say to themselves, "If I took over, I know I could do better than that."

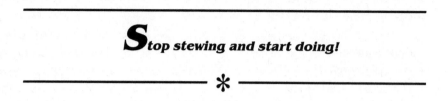

*S*top *stewing and start doing!*

✳

But the most prevalent—and overlooked—fear of all may be the fear of being successful. Most people (and this includes many executives) fear success because success carries added responsibility that may seem too heavy to bear. Success requires setting an example of excellence, which calls for risk and effort. It is tempting to believe the myth to play it safe instead of stepping out to do it now and do it right.

QUALITY IS JOB ONE!

Buzzwords of American industry in the late seventies through the mid eighties have been *quality* and *quality control*. Ford became famous for its TV commercials trumpeting, "Quality Is Job One!" And Ford's current trend of increased earnings in the face of tough competition is testimony that *quality* is more than a word for a slogan.

Philip Crosby's book, *Quality Is Free: The Art of Making Quality Certain,* helped set the pace for American industry's new pursuit of excellence by introducing tools such as the Quality Management Maturity Grid, the zero-defects concept, and the fourteen-step Quality Improvement Program.

His innovations and ideas were applied in many companies, particularly the ITT Corporation where he served for fourteen years as corporate vice president and director of quality control. Employing 350,000 workers, and with yearly sales of over $15 billion, ITT set out to make itself the standard for quality worldwide. By using Crosby's concepts, the corporation reduced its manufacturing costs, as well as service, warranty inspection, and reworking costs, by an amount equivalent to 5 percent of sales. In 1968, ITT saved $30 million. By 1976, $530 million.

Philip Crosby got his start in quality control as a junior technician testing fire control systems for B-47's. After four or five years of battling mistakes, errors, and apathy, he hit upon a basic principle that has dictated his approach to quality ever since: "Why spend all this time finding and fixing and fighting when you could prevent the incident in the first place?"[2] In other words, get everyone thinking the same thing: *I do things right—the first time.*

These days companies large and small are concerned about quality. Initially developed by W. Edwards Deming in the late 1940s, the quality circle concept was shipped from the United States to Japan. That country improved on it and brought it back to the States where it finally became popular in the 1960s and 1970s. In 1986 Patrick Townsend published *Commit to Quality*, a book that refined the quality circle into the quality team.

Prior to joining the Paul Revere Insurance Company in the fall of 1983, Townsend had spent twenty years in the Marine Corps where he learned many valuable lessons in doing it right the first time. One of his more revolutionary concepts was to get everyone in the company involved in the quality team process instead of having volunteers participate in a quality circle. In 1984, the first year of using Townsend's Quality Has Value Program, Paul Revere was able to save $8.5 million.[3]

It's obvious that quality pays in the business world. I believe it also pays in personal life. I have always been a strong believer in quality— doing quality work, giving quality service, and purchasing quality products and services.

I believe quality is like a two-sided gold coin. One side of quality includes doing the right things and doing them right the first time. That is how to stay out from under the gun. It's a marvelous time-saver, problem preventer, and relationship builder.

The other side of the gold coin of quality involves a willingness to invest money in what lasts longer and serves better. There is usually a definite relationship between quality and cost, but those who buy things only because of the impressive price tag are missing the real point.

It's far better to buy something because of how much it is *worth*. Buy the quality car, not because you want to impress your neighbor, but because it will last longer and give you a better and safer ride. Buy the handmade item of clothing, not because of its label, but for its better fit, wearability, and style.

Quality Is Smart is not a Yuppie slogan. It's a truth to practice every day. If you had to make a parachute jump, where would you shop to get outfitted? Would you buy your chute at a discount store or the flea market? When shopping for something on which your life would depend, would you look for a bargain, or would you go to the expert with the best reputation and a price to match?

That's what quality is all about. Quality means you can pull the rip cord, press the button, or turn on the engine and know that what you're counting on will work again and again and again.

To be the best you can be, commit to reaching your goals by always doing quality work and making a quality effort in everything you undertake.

BREAKING OUT OF THE PROCRASTINATION RUT

I've included some action steps for moving from procrastinating to proactivating. You might find it easier to tackle one or two at a time and work up to implementing all ten.

1. Set your wake-up time a half hour early tomorrow, and leave it at the earlier setting. Use this time to think about the best way to spend your day.

2. Memorize and repeat this motto: Action TNT—Action Today, Not Tomorrow. Handle each piece of incoming mail only once, and block out specific times to initiate phone calls, to receive incoming phone calls, and to meet people in person.

3. Give solution-oriented feedback when people tell you their problems. Ask, "What's the next step?" or "What would you like to see happen?"

4. Concentrate all your energy and intensity, without distraction, on the successful completion of your current major project. Finish what you start.

5. Instead of participating in group griping, pity parties, or grudge collecting, single out someone or something to praise. Instead of being unhelpfully critical, be constructively helpful.

6. Limit your television viewing to mostly enlightening, educational, special shows. Watch news programs on a need-to-know basis, and don't make the sensational 11:00 P.M. headlines the input you go to sleep with each night.

7. Make a list of five necessary but unpleasant projects you have been putting off. Put a completion date after each project. Immediate

action on unpleasant projects reduces distress and tension. It is very difficult to be active and depressed at the same time.

8. Seek out and talk, in person, to a successful role model and mentor. The most productive people are ones who learn from the successes and setbacks of others. Modeling is looking at other people's lives, interviewing them, listening to them, and really finding out how they do it right.

9. Understand that FEAR is False Education Appearing Real and that LUCK is Laboring Under Correct Knowledge. The more information you have on any subject, especially successful case histories, the less likely you will be to put off your decisions.

10. View problems as normal indications of change in progress. Since society and business are changing rapidly, it's up to the individual to view change as normal and to see many of the changes taking place as positive rather than negative.

With this proactive approach, you escape the clutches of procrastination and drive out the specter of fear of success. Most important you banish the myths of whatever will be will be. Like Annie, you love tomorrows because they are only a day away. You wake up saying, "Whatever will be *won't* be . . . if it's to be, it's up to me!"

TURN MOTIVATION INTO MOTIVE-ACTION

When you stop to think about it, there is no such thing as a future decision. You face only present decisions that will affect what will happen in the future. Procrastinators wait for just the right moment to decide. If you wait for the perfect moment, you become a security seeker who is running in place, going through the motions, and getting deeper in a rut.

If I wait for every objection to be overcome, I will attempt nothing. My personal motto is, Stop Stewing and Start Doing. I can't be depressed and active at the same time. I like changing the word *motivation* slightly to reflect a personal commitment to take charge of today and make it the best day I can: Motive plus action equals motive-action.

Everybody is looking for new ways to get motivated. Companies and corporations pay sizable fees to consultants who try to make their personnel more productive and fire up their sales people. A motivated person thinks, *I'm going to try it*. But motivation must turn into motive-action, or nothing will happen. That is the quandary of the poet who wrote:

> I spent a fortune
> On a trampoline,
> A stationary bike
> And a rowing machine
> Complete with gadgets
> To read my pulse,
> And gadgets to prove
> My progress results,
> And others to show
> The miles I've charted—
> But they left off the gadget
> To get me started![4]

The gadget that can get you started is motive-action. Try it and see!

*

PARABLE FOR PROCRASTINATORS

This is a story about four people named Everybody, Somebody, Anybody, and Nobody. There was an important job to be done, and Everybody was sure that Somebody would do it. Anybody could have done it, but Nobody did it. Somebody got angry about that because it was Everybody's job. Everybody thought Anybody could do it, but Nobody realized that Everybody wouldn't do it. It ended up that Everybody blamed Somebody when Nobody did what Anybody could have done.

CHAPTER 9

*P*ASSION, PRACTICE AND PERSEVERANCE____

"BEGUN IS HALF-DONE," as they say, but what about the other half? Perhaps the hardest task is to discipline yourself to keep going when things don't work out, when difficulties and frustrations flood in from every direction.

A personal success story shared by Patti Benedict, who lives in Jackson, Mississippi, provides an excellent example of self-discipline at its best. She opened her letter to me by saying she had been applying principles from one of my audiotape albums with real benefit. Then she shared the following odyssey:

> Early in May, while riding bicycles through an elegant subdivision, my companion and I passed a house that appeared abandoned. Curious, we walked around it and saw that it had been devastated in the upper rear level by a fire; the damage was not noticeable from the street. As we walked through the house, we noted its charred and smoke-blackened interior, the ruined flooring, and my companion commented: "You know, a couple of really dedicated people could restore this place."
>
> His eyes twinkled. We have worked together on projects at our office before, and had been dating for a short time when this occurred. He had no way of knowing he had struck at my deepest fantasy from childhood—to restore a house. I knew it was a doable project.
>
> By the next day I had tracked down the owners to their out-of-state location, and here began the team effort which always marked

projects Rod and I worked on. He dealt with the owners and I took on the bankers. It was the most positive, "winner" of an experience I've had in years.

First was homework. Insurance reports, photographs, appraiser's analysis, and more went into the files. (I might add that at this point friends were already branding us as "crazy.")

The first banker I went to see told me he was amazed at the amount of research I had done. (He asked if I was a realtor!) For every question, I had an answer. I laid out before him a room-by-room analysis of work needed, estimated cost, the schedule for doing the work, resources available and those required. He told me "no one comes in here this prepared!"

He was genuinely apologetic when his board, upon seeing the house, pronounced it "too risky" and backed out. He told me not to give up and referred me to another banker who was very real estate oriented. Undaunted, I went to see him and described the project. He also told me he was thoroughly impressed by my presentation. It took him five minutes to give me tentative approval.

When the board saw the house, they also got cold feet. But he believed in me, and said I could have the loan definitely *if* I also put up my own house (as collateral) until the burned one was reframed and "dry."

I never hesitated. It was an exhilarating experience to go in with a project of this magnitude, 32, divorced, and female, and WIN! (You see, I actually bought the house and secured the loan in *my name*.)

People said it couldn't be done. The house was only good for salvage. We were totally mad to take something like this on. We started working. People shook their heads. We continued working. In less than a month we had it gutted to the studs. People said, "Well, maybe it's possible, but it's so much work!"

What no one realized was that house was like my life a little over a year ago: shattered, seemingly beyond the effort required to repair and rebuild it. But I put in the effort, and built something beautiful out of my life. And I saw something just as beautiful in that house. Rod felt the same way, having experienced a painful divorce in his own life. We continued to work.

The part they said couldn't be done is now finished. The shingles go on the roof next week. The rest of it—insulation, sheetrock, fixtures—is straightforward construction work, like on any other house.

People say, "Wow, isn't that amazing," now. Yes, in some ways. No, in others. We believed in the house, in ourselves, in each other. And we learned some things working on this project together, day after day, night after night, that we might not have seen otherwise.

When the house is finished, it will be a wedding present to us. On November 15 of this year.

Maybe we should call it, "The House That Love Built."

NOTHING HAPPENS WITHOUT SELF-DISCIPLINE

Patti closed her letter with some photos of the house and a few vital statistics. The "House That Love Built" has 3,100 square feet and sits on two and one-half acres. When completed, it was appraised at $140,000 and had a final mortgage of only $70,000—what Patti calls "a WIN-WIN situation!"

I couldn't agree more! Patti's dream turned into a goal that she pursued with passionate enthusiasm. And it was the mix of self-discipline and persistence with that passion that brought her through.

In my tape albums I stress that self-discipline forces you to put your effort where your mouth is. Self-discipline begins where lip service ends. All other winning qualities are absolutely worthless without a passionate self-commitment to discipline.

Everything we've talked about so far in this book is extremely important to anyone interested in being the best. We have exploded myths about our value, our integrity, our natural gifts, and our potential. We have talked about the need for a meaningful purpose, measurable goals, and being proactive to reach those goals. But even using these tools and techniques will not give us ultimate victory. Only self-discipline can take us to the top.

SETTING PRIORITIES IS AS EASY AS *A-B-C*

I have known many people who seem very disciplined. They set a lot of goals and scurry about in constant activity, but they never accomplish much. Tragic is the life, indeed, that is busy accomplishing very little.

How, then, do you get something accomplished—something that really matters? You always check yourself to be sure that along with doing things right, you're always doing the right things at the right time. In other words, you constantly set, observe, evaluate, and reset your priorities.

There is nothing new in talking about priorities per se. All the success seminars emphasize the need for prioritizing in order to reach goals, and they offer all kinds of systems to do this. In my seminars I teach one that I think is as useful as any. I simply call it *A-B-C*, and it works like this: I have three priority lists on cards and in a notebook. I label these priorities *A, B,* and *C*: *A* for "action immediately," *B* for "before the weekend," and *C* for "can wait." I like to use color codes: red for urgent, yellow for this week, blue for this month, and green for "when there's time." I become aware of what keeps me from completing my most important priorities, and when necessary, I rewrite my personal script to take positive action to get rid of distractions and zero in on what is really important.

As you have easily seen, the *A-B-C* system is nothing more than a glorified list. If you don't already have your own system, you may want to try this one or something similar to sort out and keep track of your priorities. But what makes something a priority? Where does a priority originate? To know that, you have to go back to how you develop your habits.

THE ANATOMY OF A HABIT

In *Seeds of Greatness,* I talked about a critical part of the brain that I call the guardian of your mind. The scientific term for this four-inch network of cells radiating from your brain stem is the *reticular activating system*—RAS for short.

Without getting too technical, let's imagine a little character posted in your mind, and in keeping with his official functions, we'll just call him RAS. RAS is the sentinel who is responsible for filtering all incoming stimuli, everything from sights and sounds to smells and touches. Nothing gets past RAS unless permission is granted. RAS determines moment by moment which information is going to become part of you. In other words, RAS is the one who is really in control of your to-do list and your priorities. RAS decides what habits you break or form.

Is RAS a tyrant who controls your life and leaves you prisoner of forces beyond your control? Absolutely not. RAS is your obedient slave—your robot, if you please. The only real question is, what do you want RAS to do? Be sure you know, because RAS has an uncanny ability to do only what is *really important to you*.

Your reticular activating system is at work in a thousand ways.

Suppose, for example, you move to a new apartment near an airport or next to the freeway or to train tracks. For a while—a few days to a few weeks—it seems as if you'll never get a good night's sleep again. But then a strange thing happens. The noise stops bothering you. You start sleeping through the night. Eventually, you don't even hear anything distracting. Friends come by to visit and ask, "How can you stand it here? I can't hear myself think!"

"Stand what?" you want to know. And you realize they mean the noise of the jets overhead or the traffic going by the window. "Oh, that," you say. "Guess I just got used to it."

Once you decided that your goal was to live in your new apartment, your RAS enabled you to get used to the noise. Living there became your real priority. The place had the room you needed, it was near work, it was across the hall from someone you wanted to meet—whatever the reason, you decided living in the apartment was more important than being bothered by the noise. And once your RAS was convinced that you were convinced, it filtered out the noise, and you didn't "hear anything" any more.

YOUR RAS ACCEPTS NEGATIVE OR POSITIVE INPUT

As I said, your reticular activating system never tells you what to do. You are in charge, and it does only what you ask. It will take negative or positive input, and the only thing it is concerned about is how important that input is to you.

Do you know someone who seems stuck in a failure syndrome or who is accident-prone? If you do, you've probably heard one of these explanations for such a plight: "I guess I'm just unlucky" or "I guess it's fate" or "I'm just a klutz, I guess."

The RAS of this individual would say, "Fiddlesticks! It's what you have programmed me to tune in on. You have sent me direct orders to block out all the positive thoughts that could lead you to success, and you want me to let in all the negative stuff you say you're trying to avoid."

The reverse can be true. The RAS can be programmed to tune in on success instead of failure. If someone wants to wake up at 5:00 A.M. to go on a special fishing trip, the RAS will see to it without any clock radios or jangling bells.

The reticular activating system explains why some people are accident-prone and others are success-prone. It explains why some people see a problem in every suggested solution and others see a solution for every problem.

Remember, your RAS isn't interested in what you tell other people to make an impression, keep up a front, or offer an excuse. Your RAS is interested in what is really important to you, and *your RAS can always tell*. What is dominating your thinking? Whatever it is, your RAS will take you in that direction, just as surely as the Mississippi flows to the Gulf of Mexico.

MY RAS BECAME A "BOATAHOLIC"

I know what I'm talking about, because I was a willing victim of my own RAS nearly twenty years ago. One Saturday afternoon I was browsing around the marinas near San Diego's Mission Bay with my family, and I became fascinated with all the activity around the cabin cruisers and sailing yachts. *How magnificent*, I thought to myself. *That's the life! We could live aboard our boat. I could move my office aboard and I could write off half the yacht as a business expense. I could go after the big albacore off the Coronado islands. Maybe our children could all get jobs around the docks to help amortize the loan.* These magnificent obsessions were steaming through my mind at about 31 knots!

What I didn't realize at the time was that my RAS was listening, processing, and recording. When we got home, he made me look at the "Boats for Sale" want ads in the newspaper. I wasn't really seriously considering buying an expensive cabin cruiser, but my RAS was underlining several ads with a red marking pen. "This is ridiculous," I moaned. "I can't even afford a Boston Whaler and here I am clipping want ads for 40-, 50-, and 60-footers." My RAS wasn't listening to my whining. He was busy visualizing a glassy ocean, a cool breeze, and a marlin chair.

The following Saturday, I had planned to mow the lawn, trim the hedge, and clean the garage. But instead, my RAS made me drive to the marina—without my family—and take a demonstration cruise off La Jolla with a professional yacht broker. The yacht broker's RAS obviously was programmed to sell me the world's biggest boat. All I remember is hearing the salesman say, "Put this captain's hat on, get behind those throttles on the flying bridge, and head out through the breakwater!"

How was I going to explain to my wife that I had gone down to the garden section of Sears for a new pair of hedge clippers and had come back with a 70-foot motor cruiser with twin diesels, a washer/dryer, a color TV, a teak master bedroom suite, a rosewood conference table, and a skeet-shooting range on the aft salon deck?

But that's exactly what happened. I was now a proud owner of *The Minnie Lee*, a beautiful 70-foot, retrofitted British PT boat that had been transformed into an ocean cruising yacht with a 2500-mile range. Before my family could recover from their absolute state of shock, I, my RAS, and a few adventurous partners set sail for Costa Rica in search of the one billion dollars' worth of silver bars known as the Treasure of San Martin.

As we steamed past El Salvador bound for Cocos Island, a few hundred miles off the coast of Puntarenas, Costa Rica, I felt a sudden seizure of buyer's remorse and was flooded with feelings of guilt. *What am I doing here on this crazy, Don Quixote safari?* I sat bolt upright in my hammock, which I had strung beneath the covered salon just aft of the skeet shooting area, and nearly fell overboard. *How am I going to PAY for all this?* I yelled to myself, loud enough to get my RAS's attention. My RAS replied matter of factly, *I don't have to pay for your goals. I just get them for you. You have to figure out how to pay for them.* And my RAS went back to thinking about the fabulous Treasure of San Martin.

We ran out of money and free time before we got to Cocos Island. We did get to Costa Rica, where we were boarded by some unscrupulous locals who threatened to confiscate the yacht unless we paid them a special "berthing fee" of twenty thousand dollars. With the assistance of the Costa Rican army, we headed north for home the next morning. As soon as we arrived back at our slip at the Islandia Hotel Marina on San Diego's Mission Bay, we put *The Minnie Lee* up for sale. Before long it was sold to a millionaire, whose financial statement matched the obsession of his own RAS.

What I learned from this bizarre but true experience is that your RAS will always steer you toward your dominant thoughts, whether or not they are good for you, and whether or not you can afford them. Whatever you credit in your thoughts as important will be manifested in some way. Take my word for it!

DON'T BREAK YOUR BAD HABITS—REPLACE THEM

Another commonly accepted myth says that you have to break a bad habit (of smoking, overeating, etc.). And along with that goes the idea of the habit's being so strong that you're hooked.

The truth is, you don't break a bad habit; you replace it with a good one. Instead of sending your RAS messages about what you don't want to be or do ("I don't want to overeat" or "I don't want to smoke"), send messages that say, "I'm getting in shape by putting the right things into my body," or "I'm really a size seven, and in another two months all my clothes will be, too!"

What is your target? The only way you will reach it is to make the behavior you want part of your life—that is, make it part of your habits. Do you want better forehand in tennis? Get the proper instruction, and keep hitting that forehand over and over again.

PRACTICE, THEN PRACTICE SOME MORE

I love the old story about the young violinist who dashed up to the cabby, violin case in hand, breathlessly panting, "Quick! How do I get to Carnegie Hall?"

The cabby eyed him and his violin case and responded, "Practice, man, practice."

What is your Carnegie Hall? Where are you headed? How are you practicing to get there? What habits are you forming?

Perhaps you see someone doing something different—something stimulating and "adult." Maybe you watch it on television or in a movie, and you see it done at a party or at the office. You like what you see, and you want to do it, too. Or perhaps you want to fit into the group because "everybody's doing it." So you emulate and imitate, and the seemingly harmless act of playing copycat grows, thought upon thought, act upon act, until it is conditioned into a steel cable that can either strengthen or shackle your life.

Everyone learns the same way: by observation, imitation, and repetition. Harmful habits, such as self-criticism, smoking, excessive drinking, overeating, laziness, depression, tardiness, and insensitivity, are learned and developed into character traits through relentless, self-disciplined practice.

In the same way, helpful and successful habits of high self-esteem, substance avoidance and control, proper nutrition, dedication, enthusiasm, reliability, and empathy for others are also learned, internalized, and retained through relentless practice. The positive approach to a problem is much more likely to succeed than the negative one. It is far easier to start doing something new than to stop doing something that has become a long-standing routine.

For example, suppose you are a heavy smoker and finally decide the slogan is right: A Pack a Day Takes Ten Years Away! So you try the following program:

1. Commit yourself to clean lungs and a healthier heart.

2. Enroll in a reputable smoking cessation clinic or program.

3. Put sugarless mints or gum where the cigarettes used to be, in the car, in your desk drawer, in a pocket, and so on.

4. Become aware of your new habit of reaching for, unwrapping, and putting a mint or piece of gum in your mouth.

5. Write down and often repeat new scripts about yourself, such as: I am in control of my habits and my health . . . I am fit for life . . . my lungs are clean and strong . . . I breathe in only fresh air . . . my stamina and endurance are increasing . . . the nutritional meals I eat taste even better now.

6. Listen to positive audiotape affirmations specifically designed to develop a smoke-free attitude.

7. Congregate in smoke-free areas of buildings and transportation vehicles.

8. Enjoy the feelings, sights, and sounds of your new state of health.

9. Surround yourself with nonsmokers.

10. Enjoy your heightened sense of smell, taste, health, and appearance.

The truth is, you don't break a bad habit; you replace it with a good one

---
✳

By practicing the ten steps outlined here, you will be applying a basic principle: it is difficult to do two things at the same time. Instead of continuing your old habit of smoking, *you will be replacing it with a new habit*. As you get involved in new actions and attitudes, they replace the old ones. With all these new activities going on, you won't have time for your old bad habits. People often talk about going "cold turkey" to break a habit. I prefer going "warm turkey" and replacing the old bad habit with a new good one.

Anyone who has ever achieved anything can give credit to practice. And we all practice every day in one way or another. The trouble is, most of us spend time practicing our bad habits rather than our good ones.

It has taken me many years to set aside regular periods during the day for prayer and giving thanks to our Lord for all the blessings He has bestowed upon me and my family. Beyond saying grace at mealtimes and during worship services at church, I have set a specific time in the morning and again at night to express my devotion to Him. Even prayer is habit forming.

SELF-DISCIPLINE DOES WITHIN WHILE YOU DO WITHOUT

Master actors and actresses do not trust luck, inspiration, or willpower to do well in a performance. They consider each role as the most important one. They put every ounce of concentration and excellence into the current part. They rehearse their lines over and over. To bring their art to a live audience from the stage or to the all-seeing eye of the camera, they become experts in self-discipline.

I often tell my seminar audiences that self-discipline means doing within while you do without. Exactly what does that mean? The answer has two parts:

1. Doing within while you do without means being able to focus mentally on your goal while you do without certain things to reach that goal. You may have to go without sleep, rest, that relaxing television show you want to watch, or that ice-cream sundae you're just dying to devour.

2. But in another sense, as you keep doing something mentally within, you will eventually be able to do it without—that is, on the outside. You will be able to realize your goal physically, materially, and visibly.

Every four years we have the opportunity to watch Olympians who are almost flawless examples of continued practice that builds good habits. A key to their success is their ability to focus on what they want to become—the best runner or swimmer or gymnast or whatever. Before they can compete in their sport with such tremendous skill and strength, they have to mentally simulate the correct way of doing it and then practice over and over again.

Do you want to be the best you can be? The secret of winning is practicing flawless technique that you learn from a coach or mentor with a proven track record of success. And as you practice within, you learn to discipline your thoughts to create a new habit of superb performance.

LEARNING FROM LITTLER'S PICTURE-PERFECT GOLF SWING

When I was a scrawny kid in junior high, I'd pick up spending money by caddying at the La Jolla Country Club. I'd carry two bags for two dollars over eighteen holes, and then I'd earn another dollar for the day by shagging balls on the practice range.

Another kid there—about two years ahead of me at La Jolla High—didn't go out to shag balls. He went to hit them as he took golf lessons from the master club pro, Paul Runyan, who some have called the greatest golf teacher of all time. Paul Runyan taught Gene Littler his perfect golf swing. And guess who sometimes shagged Gene Littler's golf shots as he hit hundreds of them at the 60-, 75-, and 100-yard markers?

The first few times I took my little leather bag and went out to shag balls for Gene, I fully expected to be running all over the place. That's the way most golfers I caddied for played. But even as a young teenager, Gene Littler could hit the ball with incredible precision. He literally would hit those golf balls right into my bag or put them close enough for me to reach in a step or two!

Gene's scenario for success was simple but effective. He had tremendous natural talent, but he combined that talent with a quality teacher and then added the persistent discipline of practice, practice, practice.

No wonder Gene Littler is generally acknowledged as having the perfect golf swing. Developing that swing was one of Gene's priorities, and he mastered it through constant training. Even in his teens, he practiced a truth that applies to every skill, every sport, every business, and every high-performance situation in life:

YOU'VE GOT TO LEARN THE RIGHT MOVES BEFORE YOU PLAY THE GAME

Gene Littler learned the right moves, and he continues to play the game brilliantly. In the "twilight" of his PGA career he joined the senior tour where he has won any number of major tournaments. He also has won a battle with cancer. Several years ago, Gene discovered cancer in the lymph nodes beneath one arm. When the surgeons removed the tumor, they also had to take some of the muscles from the arm. After a long recuperating period and endless hours of disciplined therapy, Gene came back to display that marvelous swing and win a major PGA event.

Another great quality about Gene Littler is his consideration of others. His priorities go far beyond a perfect golf swing. He is one of the very best family men I have ever met. He is known by his friends and colleagues as Gentleman Gene Littler. I can think of no one who is more respected in his community and among his colleagues. I have never heard of an arrogant word coming from his mouth.

Gene Littler is what I call a total or complete man. He matched his inner value with integrity and self-respect. He discovered his potential and natural gifts and pursued his goals with consistent self-discipline. He learned the right moves, and then he played the game with distinction and excellence.

WHY SOME OF THE MOST TALENTED NEVER MAKE IT

Some of the most talented singers are never heard. Some of the most talented writers are never read. Some of the most talented athletes never make a team. Why? Because they don't develop their gifts into a quality, disciplined performance. They look for the shortcut, the easy way; they think they can deliver quality without paying the price in the practice arena. They want success without discipline.

I have interviewed some of the happiest, most productive people in the world and have found in them a combination of enjoyment of work and appreciation for excellence. They realize that because most of their adult lives are spent working, they might as well enjoy it.

Unfortunately, in many circles, excellence is almost frowned upon. The celebrity who gets busted for drug use becomes a hero, while employees who work long and hard are often ridiculed and resented.

The masses cheer when someone wins a million dollars playing the lottery, but they hold ambivalent feelings toward the individual who prospers through his own efforts. Often, they wonder if he cheated, if he was just plain lucky, or if somebody gave him financial help. One way or another, they dismiss him as a thorny reminder of what they could be if they had not embraced mediocrity.

Real success—being the best you can be—is not in the stars or the luck of the draw. It is in persistent, daily effort. Consider these startling findings from the National Sales Executives Association concerning sales persistence. I hope you are as amazed and as impressed as I am.

- Eighty percent of all new sales are made after the *fifth* call to the same prospect.

- Forty-eight percent of all sales persons make one call, then cross off the prospect.

- Twenty-five percent quit after the second call.

- Twelve percent of all sales representatives call three times, then quit.

- Ten percent keep calling until they succeed.

And what does being in this Top 10 Percent Club mean? These persistent sales reps are among the highest-paid people in the country, along with a few celebrities, corporate executives, and professionals. The 10 percent who persist get the real payoffs.

SELF-DISCIPLINE TAKES TIME—AND MORE TIME

At the center of effective self-discipline is the use of time. I have always tried to make the most of my time, but like anyone else, I have those days when it seems as if all my efforts have been wasted. The good news is that no matter how much time I have wasted in the past, I still have all of tomorrow and the tomorrows after that. When I realize the past hour has been wasted, I refuse to continue wasting my time with fretting and stewing. I remember I still have the next hour to start setting priorities and doing what I choose to do.

One of my favorite quotations is Horace Mann's lost-and-found advertisement:

> Lost, one 24-hour, 24-carat golden day. Each hour studded with 60 diamond minutes. Each minute studded with 60 ruby seconds. But don't bother to look for it. It is gone forever; that wonderful, golden day, I lost today.

Horace Mann didn't believe in killing time. Neither should you, because you are really killing opportunities for success. To manage the time better in your life and ensure success, try these proven techniques:

Use a self-development plan. Write down the knowledge you require, the behavior patterns you are changing, and the improvements you desire in your life and work. And keep your plan updated. Star the items you have achieved, and add others to your list. Daily refer to the list for positive reinforcement.

Begin each day with a question. What are you going to accomplish today that is the best use of your time? What will lead you a step closer to your greater purpose? When faced with a decision involving your time, ask yourself: Does this action substantially help me toward achieving my goals?

Learn from good role models. Seek out and talk to people who are currently doing what you want to do most and who are doing it well. Learn everything you can from them. Determine the steps they took, their planning procedures, and how they overcame obstacles and setbacks.

***S**elf-discipline means doing within while you do without*

--------------------------- ✳ ---------------------------

Use the unpleasant to develop self-discipline. Make a monthly list of five necessary but unpleasant jobs you have been putting off. Estimate how long it will take to do each job, and set aside time to complete it. You normally won't complete all five in one day or even one week, but don't be concerned about that. What is important is starting and finishing each task. Taking immediate action on unpleasant projects reduces stress and tension and frees you to move ahead with your positive priorities.

MOVE FROM ALSO-RAN TO WINNER'S CIRCLE

The above techniques are basic and obvious, but they have helped me move from an also-ran up to the winner's circle. Staring at the compelling distractions on a TV screen is one of the major wastes of time I have battled in my life. The average American adult spends nearly thirty hours per week in a semistupor escaping from the priorities and goals that are never really set. I have learned to enjoy and benefit from the very best TV has to offer in about seven total viewing hours each week.

It would take one hundred lifetimes to accomplish all you are capable of doing. If you had forever, you would not need to set goals, plan carefully, and choose directions. As you have seen, the reticular activating system is one of the mind's most fascinating features. You can program your RAS with dominant thoughts repeated vividly over and over again. That way you can filter out the unimportant distractions and concentrate on what will lead to success. I call it overriding.

Many people think they can erase what they have learned. But you can't erase your thoughts; you can only override them with new thoughts that are habitually repeated until they become new dominant thoughts—your magnificent obsession.

I can never escape or outgrow my habits. I can only replace them with new ones through constant practice. I never pay attention to statements or thoughts that describe a bad habit I want to break. I pay attention only to input describing the good habits I want to develop and retain. The positive new habits are the ones I practice to replace the old ones. This is a simple psychological technique called habit substitution.

Making a habit of setting worthwhile goals and of practicing winning lifestyle actions to support these goals is a priceless gift to myself. I never stop praying for guidance, and I often examine my motives to maintain my integrity. I call it the habit of excellence. With God's help, I am becoming the scriptwriter, producer, and star of a new real-life drama that offers an exciting opportunity for fulfillment.

Instead of leaving my future to chance, peer pressure, or media brainwashing, I am directing my future by choice. You can do the same if you really want to be the best you can be.

THE POWER OF HABIT

You may know me.

I'm your constant companion.

I'm your greatest helper; I'm your heaviest burden.

I will push you onward or drag you down to failure.

I am at your command.

Half the tasks you do might as well be turned over to me. I'm able to do them quickly, and I'm able to do them the same every time if that's what you want.

I'm easily managed, all you've got to do is be firm with me.

Show me exactly how you want it done; after a few lessons I'll do it automatically.

I am the servant of all great men and women; of course, servant of the failures as well.

I've made all the great individuals who have ever been great.

And I've made all the failures, too.

But I work with all the precision of a marvelous computer with the intelligence of a human being.

You may run me for profit, or you may run me to ruin; it makes no difference to me.

Take me. Be easy with me and I will destroy you.

Be firm with me and I'll put the world at your feet.

Who am I?

I'm Habit![1]

CHAPTER 10

*T*URNING FAILURE INTO *FERTILIZER*————————

MOST BOOKS ABOUT success skip the subject of this chapter. After all, what do failure and disappointment have to do with success and being the best?

Everything.

Few people want to deal with failure and disappointment. Most prefer to believe one of the most misleading success myths of them all:

ALL YOU NEED IS A POSITIVE ATTITUDE

A positive attitude is an important part of being the best you can be, but it is only a part. It can become a superficial catchall, which leads to the emptiness and frustration of parroting ideas like this one: If I can conceive it and believe it, I'll achieve it.

A major goal of this book is to analyze the real differences between myths and truths. Sometimes the differences are obvious, even blatant. In other cases, the differences are subtle. There is a fine line between truth and myth. Some myths contain some truth, and conversely, it is not hard to twist certain truths into myths. For example, I can take the truths shared in this book and turn them into myths by uprooting them from their context and dressing them up with a little success hype: the honest man always succeeds; God don't make no junk, and He wants you to be rich; find your gift, and you'll find success; and you can build the habit of success.

These statements make success sound rather simple, but as Murphy's second law puts it,

NOTHING IS EVER AS SIMPLE AS IT SEEMS.

Reality tells us honest people can fail and often do. Yes, God gives us our inner value, but what we make out of it is our responsibility, not His. And there is no doubt we can be very gifted, but we may never develop those gifts. In short, to build the habit of success, we better know how to handle failure.

SUCCESS IS "IN" AT THE LIBRARY OF CONGRESS

Failure and disappointment are as much parts of life as success and achievement, but that couldn't be proved at the Library of Congress in Washington, D.C. A few years ago, a friend and talented colleague of mine, Gerhard Gschwandtner, publisher of *Personal Selling Power,* decided to research the subject of success there. He found 1,200 books in the success category and 220 more on winning. Only 16 titles appeared on the subject of losing.

Puzzled, Gerhard went back to the computer to see what it held on the subject of disappointment, which seemed to him to be one of the most common human experiences. He looked under three languages—English, German, and French—and found one magazine article entitled "The Management of Disappointment" by Dr. Abraham Zaleznik, which had appeared in the *Harvard Business Review* in 1967! His curiosity fully piqued, Gerhard made a pilgrimage to Cambridge, Massachusetts, to meet Dr. Zaleznik at the Harvard University Graduate School of Business Administration.

Well known as a management consultant, the good doctor was surprised that anyone would show interest in the subject of disappointment. In the sixteen years since he had written the article, no one had ever discussed it with him. He believed the reason was obvious. People perceive disappointment as a downer. They do not want to think about anything that is not uplifting and positive.

Gerhard nodded with understanding. He had already been told by numerous people that he was making a mistake by thinking of writing something on disappointment and failure. They said the readers of his *Personal Selling Power* newspaper would not respond favorably to any subject that wasn't positive.

Gerhard's instincts disagreed with the advice of his friends, however. He knew people have an interest in what drives them, and they want to understand how they can improve their performance. He went ahead with his interview of Dr. Zaleznik and prominently featured his disappointment-trap concepts on the cover of *Personal Selling Power*. That issue of the paper sold more copies than any issue to date and continued to break sales records for reprints for over another eighteen months. Some of Dr. Zaleznik's key thoughts on disappointment, which appeared in that issue include the following.

A superficial definition of *disappointment* is "wanting something and not getting it," but it goes deeper than that. When what we want is very important and valuable to us, then the disappointment can become significant, even life threatening. If the disappointment is great enough, a person may not know what to do with his feelings and can wind up committing suicide.

Two of the most common misconceptions people have about disappointment are (1) it is bad; and (2) if we are disappointed, we should never show it. We are taught to deny disappointment because it can't possibly have anything to do with success. The world loves winners, not losers.

Contrary to what a lot of people think, disappointment does not equal failure. Seen in a positive light, disappointment can always lead to growth and learning.

When faced with disappointments or failure, you can do one of two things: seek comfort or seek a solution. Perhaps the best approach is to do some of both. First, step back, stop, and obtain some comfort, but don't get trapped into just staying comfortable. Lick your wounds, so to speak, heal up, and prepare for a new effort. Then go for the solution to the problem.

To go straight to trying for the solution before getting comforted can also be a trap. You can get caught up in a kind of "workaholism" that sees you putting in long hours but not accomplishing much. Meanwhile, you aren't really facing your disappointment and possibly your rage and anger.

To resolve disappointment, Dr. Zaleznik suggests these steps:

1. Talk about your disappointment with someone intelligent and caring. Someone you can trust.

2. Write down your feelings. If you are angry, let it spill out on paper. Deal with how you really feel; don't avoid it.

3. Talk with people who have also known disappointment. Find out how they dealt with it, what they learned.

4. Read about the experiences of gifted leaders who have suffered setbacks. How did they handle them? What universal principles can you find to apply to your own situations? Among the many excellent books worth study are Erik Erikson's psychological biography of Gandhi and John Mack's study of Lawrence of Arabia.[1]

TOTALLY AVOIDING FAILURE MEANS DOING NOTHING

I'm glad Gerhard Gschwandtner went with his instincts and published Dr. Zaleznik's practical insights on handling failure and disappointment. In so doing, he did a service to anyone who has ever been concerned about success. Perhaps the most important attitude in life is not the view of what success should be, because success differs for each of us. The much more important attitude to develop is how to face failure and deal with it.

When we begin anything new, we usually have little confidence because we have not learned from experience that we can succeed. This is true in all areas: learning to ride a bike, skiing, flying a high-performance jet aircraft, closing a major sale, or teaching others. I believe that success does breed more success. I do not agree, however, that failure has to breed failure.

Some people say that failure should be avoided at all costs. But if you think it through, that cost is too high. The only way to avoid failure at all costs is to do nothing. The only trouble with doing nothing is that while you avoid failure and defeat, you also avoid victory and success.

Others say that failure is like toxic waste and to think about it at all pollutes and destroys the attitudes you need for success. I see failure not as toxic waste but as fertilizer. Farmers use manure, decomposed plants, mulch, and other substances to fertilize their crops. In much the same way, your failures and disappointments can be used to enrich the soil of your mind for the planting of seeds of success.

The way to turn failure into fertilizer is to use your errors and mistakes as a way to learn, but then dismiss those errors and mistakes from your mind. Forget the failures, and focus on future success. Use failures and disappointments only as corrective feedback to get you on target again. Keep your eye on your goal, and have faith in your ability to reach it.

THE STORY OF DOMINO'S PIZZA

One of the best role models I've found for illustrating how to handle failure and disappointment is Thomas S. Monaghan, founder, president, and chairman of Domino's Pizza, Inc. If by some faint chance you have never seen or tasted a Domino's pizza, there are 3,300 Domino's pizzerias spread across America, none of which have tables. That's because Domino's is the absolute king of home-delivered pizza—anywhere you want it, within reason, of course.

The success Domino's enjoys today grew out of the fertilizer of enough failures to bury several businesses. First, a bad partnership nearly dragged the business under in 1965. In 1968, insurance paid off only one-tenth of the loss from a $150,000 fire.

By 1970, management of the debt-ridden pizza chain was assumed by a principal creditor—a bank. Ten months later, Domino's owner, Thomas S. Monaghan, resumed control and faced over one hundred lawsuits, fifteen hundred creditors, and an overall debt of $1.5 million.

No one would have really blamed Monaghan for folding his pizza tent and quietly fading away. But he was used to disappointment and crisis. He was four years old when his father died. He had grown up in foster homes, had worked as a farm hand, a pinsetter in a bowling alley, and a newsboy. In 1970, facing overwhelming debts and problems, Monaghan didn't fold and go into bankruptcy; he dug in his heels and used his failures to fertilize new seeds of success.

Not only did Thomas Monaghan fight off the lawsuits, the creditors, and the debts, but he led Domino's back from the edge of the financial grave to the very top of the food service industry. Today Domino's rates among the fifty leading food service organizations in America and is still climbing. It is considered the second-largest pizza company in the country, the fastest-growing fast-food service, and the undisputed leader in home delivery.

In Monaghan's words, "Domino's has a single goal. Its mission: to deliver a high-quality pizza, hot, within thirty minutes at a fair price." Everything done at Domino's, says Monaghan, is centered on that goal.

When all this began in 1960, Thomas Monaghan was twenty-three years old. He and his brother bought a nondescript little pizza parlor in Ypsilanti, Michigan, a tiny community between Detroit and Ann Arbor and practically on the campus of Eastern Michigan University. Tom was already running a street corner newsstand, and he thought the pizzeria would give him additional income to use toward earning a college degree in architecture.

In a year, Tom had become sole owner of the shop, called Domi-Nick's at the time. Finally, he decided to drop out of college and make a go of the pizza parlor. A year later he added another shop near the campus of Central Michigan University, and on the first delivery run he ever made, he met his future wife, Margie, in a girls' dormitory on the Central Michigan campus.

Monaghan learned the pizza trade as he practiced it—by trial and error. The fast preparation techniques Domino's uses today were developed by Monaghan as he sweat it out in that first little pizza shop, elbow deep in flour and tomatoes, hustling to make deliveries to the college campuses before the dorms closed.

Early on, Monaghan offered five different pizza sizes, including a six-inch pie for thirty cents, a favorite snack of university students. Then came the night that someone called in during the middle of rush hour to order twelve of the tiny pizzas in one batch. That was the night Monaghan decided to sell pizzas only in twelve- and sixteen-inch sizes, and his revenue was soon up by over fifty percent.

But by far the more significant lesson that gave Domino's its major trademark today was learning that residential customers who order pizzas for delivery to their homes were far more loyal and profitable than any others.

Whatever the lesson, Monaghan pressed it into action with his trial-and-error approach. Instead of letting disappointments, and what proved to be mistaken judgment, defeat him, he adapted, changed, revamped, and adapted some more. And as he adapted, he developed the certainty and the conviction that come from experience. Today he knows what he knows because he's been there.

On a good night, a good Domino's crew can turn out a pizza in six minutes flat. Drivers follow carefully tested delivery routes over pre-mapped zones and take the hot pizza, protected in a crush-resistant, thermally insulated box, to the customer's door.

Does all this seem like too much trouble? In 1985, Domino's patrons ordered 135 million pizzas and pushed Domino's sales to more than $1 billion, which is 73 percent higher than in 1984. In 1985, 954 new Domino's pizzerias opened, an all-time record for the food service industry.

According to Monaghan, Domino's management philosophy is simply the golden rule. "Just figure out how you want to be treated yourself," he says, "and then treat others that way—your customers, your employees, your franchisees, your suppliers."

If that sounds a little too idealistic for today's harsh business world, consider the five priorities that have guided Thomas Monaghan since he was a nineteen-year-old marine, shipping overseas.

1. *Spiritual*. "What good would it do to gain the world and lose my soul?" asks Monaghan, who once aspired to study for the priesthood.

2. *Family and Social*. As important as his company is, it comes second to his family, which includes his wife and four daughters.

3. *Mental Development*. Somehow Monaghan squeezes in time to be a director of Cleary College in Ypsilanti, Henry Ford Hospital, Detroit Renaissance, and National Bank of Detroit. He always spends fifteen minutes of quiet contemplation before starting work each morning.

4. *Physical Development*. Monaghan's routine each morning includes working out on his Nautilus equipment and jogging.

5. *Financial Development*. He believes that if he takes care of the other four priorities, he will make all the money he wants and "enjoy it."

It all seems to be working. His five priorities and his golden rule philosophy of management guide him in an ambitious program to expand Domino's to ten thousand outlets by the early 1990s. Besides concentrating on growth in major metropolitan areas such as Chicago and New York, he will also shoot for the international market. Domino's pizzerias already deliver in Australia, Canada, Japan, the United Kingdom, and West Germany.[2]

NEVER IDENTIFY YOURSELF WITH YOUR FAILURES

To me, Thomas Monaghan is living proof that only one danger can arise from adversity. And that is mistaking your failures for yourself. In other words, if you identify yourself with your failures, problems, and disappointments, you will probably become a failure.

The college student who sees himself as being poor at studying will invariably find that his grades will prove him right. The person who has an image of himself as the sort of person nobody likes will soon find himself avoided at work. With his self-conscious expressions, overanxiousness to please, and perhaps unconscious hostility toward those he anticipates not liking him, he literally invites rejection. His very manner and bearing drive others away.

Whenever you identify yourself with failure, you are fair game for the myth that whispers:

YOU ALWAYS FOUL IT UP . . . YOU NEVER GET IT RIGHT . . . IT'S ALL YOUR FAULT . . . YOU'RE A FAILURE

It is absolutely amazing to see the number of people who are trapped in this kind of thinking. They tell themselves that their poor performance is proof of their failure. Tragically, it never occurs to them that the trouble doesn't necessarily lie with performance. It lies with their self-image—the negative evaluations and judgments they make of themselves.

Several psychological studies have stressed the critical need to develop a positive explanatory style rather than a pessimistic one to deal with disappointments and failures. Dr. Martin Seligman, who has spent twenty years and done over one hundred experiments with almost fifteen thousand subjects, believes the way we explain things that happen to us is far more important than what actually happens. A pessimistic explanatory style can lead to depression and illness.

---

*T*o build the habit of success, we better know how to handle failure

---
*

The phrase "pessimistic explanatory style" is simply psychological jargon meaning "negative outlook on life." For example, suppose you are late for an important business lunch. If you choose to explain your tardiness with a pessimistic, negative outlook, you say: "I'm always late . . . I never seem to get away for appointments on time . . . I'm just lousy at planning my work, I guess . . . it's all my fault."

By adopting this style for explaining your failures and disappointments, you are bound to see the glass of life as half-full—or less. Dr. Seligman says his research indicates that people using this negative style are constantly more depressed than those who use the more positive approach.[3]

Let's go back to your being late for that important lunch date and try to explain it positively. You might say: "I'm normally very punctual . . . I always keep my appointments . . . this time I got trapped in the boss's office and couldn't leave when I wanted to . . . things like this are bound to happen occasionally."

One note of caution is in order. After a failure or disappointment, never use positive reinforcement to cop out or rationalize a lack of planning, self-discipline, or effort. But when you know you have done your homework and put in a good effort, positive reinforcement is the way to handle failure and turn it into fertilizer.

In many situations you may not be able to change the immediate circumstances, but you can always change your response and your attitude. Instead of repeating the old myth that you *always* blow it, concentrate on the truth:

THAT'S NOT LIKE YOU . . . NEXT TIME YOU'LL DO IT RIGHT!

Tomorrow that same situation may come up, but instead of being trapped into believing that you *always* foul up and *never* do it right, you can have a positive approach that will give you a new power to perform successfully.

WHAT HAPPENS WHEN YOU REALLY FOUL UP?

A graphic example of how to deal with a horrible mistake is found in a refreshing new book by a successful Berkeley, California, physician who writes under the pseudonym of Oscar London. The title of the book is *Kill As Few Patients As Possible and Fifty-Six Other Essays on How to Be the World's Best Doctor* (Berkeley, Calif.: Ten-Speed Press, 1987).

In one instance, Dr. London is awakened at just after 3:00 A.M. by an emergency room doctor calling from a small hospital one hundred miles away. A patient who had driven that one hundred miles to see London the previous day has just died in the emergency room of multiple pulmonary emboli. And he has died because London missed the diagnosis! The patient's wife is put on the phone, and Dr. London has to tell her that he is sorry and that he simply didn't make the right diagnosis. Dr. London hangs up and begins "survival training."

Yes, he knows he made a terrible error. When he examined the man, he thought the profuse sweating and slight shortness of breath were symptoms of the flu. After all, the lungs sounded fine, and the chest X ray was normal. But he knows he blew it.

A week later a malpractice lawyer calls, wanting to ask a few questions. All Dr. London can do is refer him to his own lawyer and hang up. A lawsuit would be serious, but he has far more on his mind right now. No malpractice suit can extract a price greater than the one he is already having to pay.

For two weeks he wears a leaden vest of grief, but he fights his way through that grief in various ways. He seeks confidants such as friends who will listen for free or psychotherapists who will listen for a fee. He tries to stay in shape and gets eight hours of sleep each night. He eats lightly and does his best to be sharp for the few patients that he simply must see.

And he is very sure not to take a few days off. He doesn't take even one drink. He knows that one drink at a time like this can wind up being a twenty-year toot.

After all, he is a doctor. Mistakes—sometimes horrible ones—can happen to him as well as anyone else. He must keep himself in one piece while he battles what he calls the horror of human imperfection.[4]

PRACTICAL VERSUS NEUROTIC PERFECTIONISM

In his essay about the errant diagnosis, Dr. London does not mention using a lot of positive-thinking slogans on himself in those terrible days following the death of the patient. But what he does tell us reveals a positive approach to the problem. Despite carrying the weight of a terrible mistake, he takes care of himself. He finds friends he can talk to, and he refuses to flagellate his already horribly damaged conscience. As a conscientious healer, he prefers to be perfect, but he must deal with the reality of his imperfection.

I like the advice given perfectionists by James Calano and Jeff Salzman, young men who in their twenties became presidents of their own companies and who have coauthored the book *Real World 101*. Calano and Salzman observe that people can take one of two approaches to trying to be excellent professionals: practical perfectionism or neurotic perfectionism. Neurotic perfectionists are never finished, their work is never quite right, and they live with high anxiety and low productivity. When they make a mistake, they are devastated.

Practical perfectionists are committed to excellence, give attention to details, and have systematic and disciplined work habits. They recognize when their projects are finished. Perhaps they could spend a little more time on something and make it "a bit better," but they realize that it's "good enough" to achieve its purpose. If they make a mistake, they handle it rather than let it handle them.[5]

If you must be a perfectionist, be practical. In the face of all errors, mistakes, and failures, don't look back. Realize that it is normal to have an initial reaction of embarrassment, regret, anger, or remorse. But take a page from Dr. London's book, and don't let your mistake put you under its gun. Instead, take positive action, and focus on what to do next.

FOCUSING ON A TOTALED 240Z

I got a good taste of this advice when one of our daughters turned sixteen and just happened to "borrow" my new Datsun 240Z, which I had obtained after considerable stretching of our budget. I had left on a trip after giving her strict orders to not touch the keys to that new burnt orange, racy 240Z. Upon my return, I would give her lessons in operating the vehicle, but until then it was supposed to be hands off.

I took the red-eye flight to Washington, secure in the knowledge that my car would be safe until I got back. The next evening while I was at dinner with a client, I was called to the phone and got the news. My daughter had not been able to resist temptation. She had driven the 240Z to downtown La Jolla and parked it with the engine still running in front of La Jolla's most exclusive department store. Some high-school friends appeared and began asking her about the car. She decided to press the accelerator to impress them with its roar of power.

She impressed them far more than she intended. Somehow, with a skill known only to neophyte teenage drivers, the gears became engaged, and my daughter drove my new car straight through the front doors of Walker-Scott Department Store. Her momentum carried her through the glass display cases of jewelry and lingerie on past the shelves of kitchenware. She didn't come to a halt until sofa beds stopped the car in its Michelin-covered tracks.

The car was totaled, but miraculously, my daughter was uninjured and not a single store patron or clerk had ventured into the path of the hurtling car. One reason nobody was hurt was that at least my daughter's timing had been good. She had hit the doors of the store at 5:01 P.M., one minute after the last customer had left and the store had closed. Only glass doors, several aisles of goods and showcases, the car, and my daughter's composure had been shattered.

I flew home immediately and found her in the hospital where she was unhurt but being held for observation.

"Dad, I'm so sorry and so ashamed. I'll bet you're just furious, aren't you?" she whispered.

I could see she was suffering mostly from remorse, so I held her hand and reassured her by saying, "On the contrary, Sweetheart. I'm relieved and grateful that no one was hurt and that you are all right."

As she fought back the tears, my daughter asked, "What did I learn from this, Dad?"

"How to make monthly payments?" I suggested. "You'll have to pay for damage to the store and help me pay for the car. But don't worry, it should be taken care of in about three years and then we can think of another car for you. Look on the bright side—you'll get a lot of experience in financial management!"

My daughter's eyes widened with shock, but she recovered and asked me one more question: "What did *you* learn from this experience, Dad?"

"The same thing you're learning—how to handle disappointment and not let one mistake get me down. I also learned to take my car keys with me whenever I leave on a trip!"

My daughter did pay off all the debts incurred by her 240Z experience and went on to become a good driver with an excellent record. She matured into a beautiful young woman, a hard worker who is talented and service oriented. Today we still laugh about the day she parked the car in Walker-Scott's furniture department. One thing about many disappointments is that while you may feel like crying when they happen, later you will probably be able to look back and laugh. As the old preacher once said, "Things come to pass—and sure enough, they do."

WHEN DISAPPOINTED . . . PERSEVERE!

An invaluable tool for handling a mistake or a disappointment, or possibly a string of them, is the ability to persevere (see chapter 9). One of my favorite perseverers is Thomas Edison. He built upon multiple losses to finally win a place among the immortals.

We've all heard of Thomas Edison. He's the one who invented the electric light bulb and the phonograph, among other things. What many people do not know, however, is that Edison's ability to handle disappointment and failure is unparalleled in the history of science.

After trying 5,000 different materials to find a filament for the electric light, Edison's co-workers were discouraged. But did Edison look back on 5,000 failures? No, he considered it "succeeding in learning 5,000 different things that would not work!"

As famous as Edison's work with the electric light became, he had far more failures in his efforts to invent a storage battery—25,000 of them in all. When someone asked him how it felt to fail so many times, he replied again, "Failure? I'm not a failure. I now know 25,000 ways *not* to make a battery." If failure is fertilizer, Edison would have put Vigoro out of business!

To be the best you can be, never label lack of success as failure. Take advantage of the lessons you learn while losing, but then regroup and keep moving toward your objective.

FEAR AND FAILURE ARE FIRST COUSINS

To handle failure, you need to know how to handle fear. In fact, if you can deal with your fears ahead of time, you can prevent failures or at least be able to deal with problems in a more positive way.

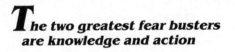

The two greatest fear busters are knowledge and action

✳

I recently came across a study done at the University of Michigan that has helped me reduce the effect of fear in my life. This study determined that 60 percent of our fears are unwarranted, and 20 percent have already become past events and are completely out of our control. Another 10 percent are so petty they don't make any difference at all. Of the remaining 10 percent of our fears, only 4 or 5 percent are real and justifiable. And we can't do anything about half of them! That means only about 2 percent of our fears are really worth thinking about, and we can solve them easily if we will simply stop stewing and start doing.

I believe the two greatest fear busters of all are knowledge and action, and I have developed a simple formula to put them both to work. Since only 2 percent of our fears are worth dealing with, I reserve 2 percent of my year—about seven days—not for fear but for follow-through. I use the seven days to deliberately concern myself with what might go wrong during the year and then follow through to make sure it doesn't. That way I can enjoy the other 358 days because I have made a special effort to make them go right.

Usually, I manage to use an entire *F* day to slay my dragons. On that one day every seven or eight weeks, I identify all the sources of current and potential worry and anxiety that might come my way. I write down my current and future concerns and list some alternative choices I might have in dealing with them.

I also use the big red *F* days to focus on one major area of my life. One of my favorites is the day I devote to fitness follow-through. I schedule my annual physical exam, which includes a body fat composition check, a blood test for cholesterol, and the usual things such as blood pressure check, chest X ray, tests for vision and hearing, and so on.

I also make sure my regular six-month dental appointments are in order. And I note how I am doing on my nutrition and diet and if I'm getting enough aerobic exercise. In short, Fitness Follow-Through Day doesn't leave me feeling concerned at all; I feel successful about my health and well-being.

Another big red *F* day is for family follow-through. Instead of worrying about not spending enough time on the family's needs, I use one full day to hear everyone out and respond to the most important worries, concerns, and desires. Of course, every day is family day at the Waitleys, but on Family Follow-Through Day, we make a special effort to be honest and open with one another. I set goals and priorities for my family that I would never set otherwise. Some of the key family outings and events that we've enjoyed have been planned during these discussions.

Some other big red *F* days include Finance, Friends, Future, and Facilities. Susan particularly likes Facilities Follow-Through Day. That's when we go over problems with the house, the office, and our vacation home. Our local repairmen also like that day because they usually get a lot of business.

As a result of my big red *F* days every seven or eight weeks, I keep up with handling major areas of responsibility and concern. I give them special periodic attention, and I take positive steps to minimize their impact. Having seven special days each year helps keep me in my usual state, which my friends describe as easygoing, mild tempered, and relaxed. Because I follow through seven or eight times a year to keep potential fears from materializing, I can think of very few things that really frighten me, that is, things that don't weigh three thousand pounds, have huge triangular teeth and cold, predatory eyes, and cut the oceans with a big dorsal fin as they stalk an overweight, middle-aged scuba diver who might be looking for abalone off shore from his beach house in northern California.

When I do venture out into the waters just off Sea Ranch, our vacation home, I often wonder if I might not look like a plump seal sushi to a shark who could wander into the area and be attracted by the slow fluttering movements of the swim fins attached to my out-of-condition legs. Every time I go abalone diving at Sea Ranch, I experience the exhilarating combination of outdoor adventure and stark (or shark?) terror. Maybe I need one more *F* day on my calendar—Fish Fear Day. Come to think of it, if I had a Fish Fear Day, I'd probably memo myself to take the following action: sell wet suit and buy abalone at the market at thirty dollars a pound and live to enjoy it! Or maybe I could talk Susan and the kids into doing the diving for me. Then I could sit on the rocks and yell, "Go for it. There's nothing to fear!"

NOTHING IS CERTAIN BUT DEATH, TAXES—AND CHANGE

The key skill needed to handle (or avoid) failure and disappointment is adaptability. They say nothing is certain but death and taxes, but one other thing you can count on is that change is constant. Every day brings shifts in the economy, the political climate, your company's stance in the marketplace, even your relationships with other family members. How you adapt to change can be your greatest challenge and also your greatest opportunity.

Science tells us that the dinosaurs failed to adapt to changing conditions and seemed to simply vanish from the earth in a relatively short period of time. They appeared eons later, however, wearing the label "Made in Detroit." When the oil shortages hit, Detroit responded to the need for compact cars that got good gas mileage with all the speed of a brontosaurus with the gout. The Japanese moved in with their Toyotas, Hondas et al., and the rest was history until Detroit came fighting back in the late seventies and early eighties.

Adaptability, or the lack of it, makes the difference between failure and success, disappointment and fulfillment. Picture, for example, a car dealership that starts selling the small Japanese compacts instead of the larger American dinosaurs. One salesman responds negatively and conveys that attitude to customers by saying, "Well, I don't suppose you really want to buy a squeaky little car like this—it's too bad we no longer handle the Super 8 X-L's." With this approach, his sales and commissions soon face extinction.

But in the same dealership, another man adapts to the new little cars from Japan. He learns all he can about them and becomes convinced that they are going to have their impact. His enthusiasm and optimism soon make him the best salesman on the floor. Eventually, he is offered a partnership.

ARE YOU AS SMART AS A BEE OR A MOUSE?

If you lack adaptability, failure and disappointment will trap you in a hopeless dead-end situation. You will be like a bee in a bottle. Bees are perfectly equipped with genetic programming and instincts for life in the hive, but they are completely at a loss when placed in a bottle with the base of the bottle turned toward a light source. Even though the other end of the bottle is open and uncapped, the bees never discover how to escape. They repeatedly fly toward the bottom of the bottle and toward the light. Being trapped in the bottle is a new situation. Somehow the light seems familiar and comforting, so they continue to try to get to it, but to no avail. Unable to adapt to their changed environment, they would eventually perish.

Mice, on the other hand, can be placed in a maze and trained to find their way to a chunk of cheese at the end. Take away the cheese and the mice will run their memorized path a few times, but then will try exploring other alternatives. They try other directions to see if they can find some cheese instead of pursuing the same route that leads to no reward.

Ironically, human beings sometimes don't show as much "smarts" as mice do. We tend to learn a set pattern that brings us certain rewards, and we continue to follow that pattern even after the rewards are removed or become only partially fulfilling. Like bees in a bottle, we keep flying toward our source of light but getting nowhere. We tend to believe the myth:

ALWAYS DO WHAT'S COMFORTABLE

This is the myth behind the old familiar excuses that pop up whenever mistakes are made, disappointment comes, something fails, or a change of some kind is obviously in order or already happening: "But we've never done it that way before." "Why tamper with what works?" "How do we know it [the needed change] will work?" "What if he is in a slump? We've got to go with what got us here." (This typical comment is made by a manager or coach who is in the World Series or the play-offs and knows that he needs to make some changes, but he's afraid to shake up his lineup.)

People who can't adapt tend to be rigid, uptight, immovable, and inflexible. Failures and disappointments paralyze them, and instead of going into action, they sit tight and hope everything will work itself out.

Persons who are willing to try to adapt are eager to implement a new approach, comfortable with taking risks, open to improvising, and willing to experiment.

What keeps individuals locked into situations that are comfortable and familiar but totally defeating and destructive? Something we looked at earlier—fear of failure. The situation calls for something to be done, a change to be made, a risk to be taken, but they seem paralyzed, frozen in place like hairy mammoths that didn't see the glacier coming.

I like the old saying that it's better to try something and fail than to do nothing and succeed. Sometimes disorderly and imperfect action is preferable to orderly, organized, sterile inaction.

Coming back to our bees-in-the-bottle analogy, instead of bees, let's try flies. Put the bottle in the same place with the bottom turned toward a bright light. Do the flies simply bounce off the bottom, futilely trying to reach the light but never escaping the bottle? On the contrary, they fly in every direction, up, down, toward the light, away from the light, bouncing against the sides of the bottle, and sooner or later they find their way out of the open neck.

The moral is clear. When you have to cope with change, disappointment, or failure, don't just stand there, do *something!* However, when something goes wrong, doing something doesn't mean pressing the panic button. Don't assume immediately that it's all your fault, that you always foul up, and that what you're doing can't work. Instead, keep your focus on the desired result.

Don't lament the past or wring your hands. Plan your strategy for your next step. Never look back at a mistake. Learn what you can from the mistake, and move on to make a tiny step forward toward success. Always reinforce your steps of success, and concentrate on the rewards of success.

Learn the lessons you need to learn from difficult and even destructive confrontations and failures. Try not to repeat those same situations again if at all possible.

Above all, set internal standards for excellence. Accept yourself as you are, but keep upgrading your standards and adapting your behavior to the situation. And remember:

THE ABILITY TO ADAPT IS EVERYTHING

＊

THE ADAPTABLE ATTITUDE IN ACTION

The following five suggestions will help you put an adaptable attitude into action:

1. Instead of fearing change, expect it. View change as normal. Constantly check yourself for how flexible you are to new ideas, surprises, and other situations that demand adaptability to change.
2. Use the salvage-the-situation approach. When things don't work out just the way you planned, don't panic or go into a blue funk. No matter what game you're playing, one loss doesn't make a season. One strikeout doesn't mean you can't win the batting championship.
3. Ignore the little disappointments and irritations in order to reach your larger goal. Many people let the little things get to them and ruin their performance, attitude, and chances for success. Adaptable people learn to live with a certain amount of inconvenience, embarrassment, discouragement, dismay, and antagonism. They concentrate on what really counts—the major goal or objective.
4. Develop your innovation techniques. According to Peter Drucker, when you are buffeted by change and faced daily with new threats and challenges, innovation is vital. There are always ways to do things more effectively. Perhaps you need to combine some old techniques with some new approaches. For ideas, see *Winning the Innovation Game* (Old Tappan, N.J.: Revell, 1986), which I coauthored with Robert Tucker.
5. Remember the prayer of Reinhold Niebuhr: change what you can, accept what you cannot change, and ask for the wisdom to know the difference.

CHAPTER 11

A FIVE-STAR RATING

EVERY YEAR I receive the new listing with eager anticipation. Because I have been traveling all over the world virtually every week for the past ten years, to nearly every major city in the United States and to many countries, I enjoy seeing which restaurants and hotels are among the chosen few to receive the coveted five-star rating. Getting five stars means the establishment consistently offers the finest quality and service available.

People can be rated in much the same way. If you have inner value, why would you not consistently offer everyone you meet the finest quality effort and the most gracious attention to service within your power? Our "adopted" daughter from Mexico is my idea of a five-star person.

Graciela Gonzalez came from the small town of El Chante about 150 miles south of Guadalajara, Mexico, to join our family when she was just seventeen. She journeyed to the United States seeking work, education, and opportunity. In her home in Mexico, she had been one of thirteen children whose parents were farmers making a meager living off the land. Watching too much TV had not been one of Graciela's problems! She had other more pressing concerns, such as how to get to California to find a job so she could send money home to help the rest of the family.

Graciela spoke no English at first and was extremely shy, but she wanted to work, to help, to seek, and to learn. In exchange for room and board, education, and an allowance, she helped us care for our younger children. In no time, she won our hearts and became, for all practical purposes, our adopted daughter.

Graciela's story is like a *Pygmalion West*. At first she would spend her free hours by herself in her room or with her other friends who had gained temporary visas from Mexico to work in the United States. She didn't want to be a bother, and she always wanted to make certain she didn't interfere with our inner family circle. We kept telling her, "Your place is here with us in the family circle." We always treated her with love and respect, and she always gave us more reasons to respect and love her.

Our Latin American Eliza Doolittle took us at our word. In the ten years we spent together, she learned fluent English and grew into a lovely young woman who gained the self-esteem that comes from realizing inner worth and finding self-respect in living a life of integrity. She went to night school, got a high-school diploma, and then went back to the University of Guadalajara where she graduated with distinction after earning a teaching degree and a professorship.

Today Graciela is in the process of becoming a U.S. citizen and is qualifying to become a bilingual teacher in the California school system. I was proud to walk her down the aisle and give her away when she married an American engineer, just as I have taken that same walk with our daughters Debbie and Dayna, and just as I hope to do with our daughters Kimberlyn and Lisa. Graciela and her husband, Ron, live with their three sons in Carlsbad, California, near the San Onofre nuclear power plant where he has an engineering position.

Her husband calls her Grace, the English equivalent of Graciela, and never was a name more appropriate. From the day I met Graciela, she displayed grace and graciousness that were unique. Graciela was always appreciative of even the smallest favor or opportunity to better herself. She was thankful for everything and showed it while in our home as well as after leaving us. Every card or letter we sent was answered. Birthdays and holidays have been remembered. She has never lost touch with us and never stopped displaying a reciprocal graciousness that was an example to us all.

Susan and I visited Graciela recently, and as she showed us through their charming home, we talked about her life. She said, "We've come a long way, haven't we?" It was just like Graciela to say "we." She has always realized the importance of others, always appreciated everyone and everything in her life.

Graciela Gonzalez made the most of what life gave her. I see her as a shining example of the "something" that is always present in someone who truly understands being the best. That something is hard to describe. The words *thankful, grateful, appreciative, considerate,* all come to mind. But other elements fit in, such as a sense of responsibility and duty to the very opportunity offered by life itself. Above all, there is the willingness to pay value to self and others because of the awareness of the beauty and wonder of living life in the here and now.

GRACIOUSNESS IS NOT GRACIOUS LIVING

No study of being the best is complete without a look at graciousness, which is not the same as the gracious living portrayed in exclusive, slick magazines filled with four-color photos of beautifully set tables adorned with freshly cut flowers. I enjoy beautifully set tables and freshly cut flowers, too, but I also know that gracious livers are not always gracious. By graciousness, I mean the personal attitudes and convictions that always remind us of where we have come from and whose shoulders we stand on to be where we are now.

The poet was right; none of us is an island. We are all linked inseparably by our need for one another. The myth tries to be convincing by declaring,

YOU ARE A SELF-MADE SUCCESS

but the truth laughs softly. No one is self-made. We all owe our advances and accomplishments to someone or something that has been a good Samaritan or Jiminy Cricket along the way. Deep down we all know this truth:

SUCCESS IS A TEAM EFFORT

For that matter, life is a team effort. The myth says, "For every winner, there must be a loser." The truth assures, "For every real winner, there must be other winners involved." The myth says, "Success is a status achieved by the few." The truth asserts, "Success is a way of life enjoyed by many, especially those who live with grace, not by the law of the jungle."

But what does graciousness mean in practical, daily terms? It is a universal quality that could take an entire book in itself to describe. But at the very least it means answering several basic questions honestly, with no pretense, cynicism, or plastic positive-thinker's platitudes. Those questions include the following: Do you know who you really are? Do you appreciate what you really have? Are you living at the right pace for you? Do you go that extra mile every day? Do you compete, or do you cooperate?

Being your best involves all the above and much more. Being your best means moving through at least four stages of maturity, and the level of maturity characteristic of each stage is made evident by these brief comments: (1) can't somebody else handle it?; (2) I can handle it; (3) please help me; and (4) please let me help you.

When you reach the fourth stage, you are flirting with graciousness. The late Lloyd Conant, the audiotape pioneer who built my speaking career and who was the most gracious man I ever knew, told me: "The very best people in the world will never be known by many. They do not seek publicity nor waste their time with vanity. Since they lead exemplary, healthy lives, they are rarely covered by the media, who tend to focus mostly on the sensational, the controversial, and the bizarre. Once in a while they make history, usually if they are in world leadership positions."

Whether or not you make history is really not important. But living graciously is important to a fulfilled, successful life.

DO YOU KNOW WHO YOU REALLY ARE?

As we saw in chapter 2, understanding your God-given inner worth is basic to self-esteem. On the hierarchy of self-esteem the *internalist* stands tallest saying, "I judge myself by internal standards, not the opinions of others. I give life my best. I apply my full value to what I do. I enjoy living."

With goals, knowledge, hard work, persistence, and adaptability, it's possible to get what you want in life. The challenging part is enjoying yourself once you have it. Executives with corner offices overlooking a magnificent city skyline may never take time to look out the window. They are caught up in real-life "Monopoly," trying to figure out how much is enough. Successful business executives own fabulous homes in the country or by the ocean, but they only go to those homes to eat and sleep. They are busy playing "king of the mountain," but the mountain keeps getting taller.

The secret of reaping the greatest benefits from hard work and purposeful living is smelling the roses while you're on the journey; don't wait until you reach the destination. You can work six days a week to provide for your family, but in the meantime your kids grow up and have children of their own, and you won't know them very well either. You can work for thirty years without a real vacation, only to discover that when you retire you won't know how to water ski, scuba dive, mountain climb, or hang glide, not to mention just sit on a rock to relax. It is all too easy to swallow the myth:

LIFE IS A RACE TO FINISH FIRST

I've often heard that the two great tragedies of life are (1) never having a great dream to strive for, and (2) never fully reaching it. The greatest tragedy, however, is reaching what you think you've been striving for only to find that it doesn't satisfy. Life isn't a race to finish first. The truth is:

LIFE IS A PROCESS TO MAKE LAST

When you know who you really are, happiness is associated more with the experience of your journey than with the fleeting moment of recognizing that you have "arrived." Success is the process of learning, sharing, and growing. Every completion points to a new beginning.

In the autumn of life, the *internalist* can look back and reflect, "I have enjoyed most of the miles and days of the journey." The *materialist,* the *achiever,* and even the *altruist* may have to look back and admit, "I worked myself to the bone, and now I'm too tired to enjoy the fruits of my labors. Is this all there is?"

AMERICA'S RICHEST MAN IS A TRUE SUCCESS

A man who has combined great wealth with real and unassuming success is Sam Walton. *Forbes* magazine once proclaimed him the richest man in America. The source of Walton's vast wealth is Wal-Mart, his chain of discount general stores that was expected to top $11 billion in sales in 1986. His annual salary as cofounder and chief executive officer of the 900-odd Wal-Mart stores, which extend through twenty-two states, is a "modest" $300,000 a year. But *Forbes* concluded that his total family holdings and stock dividends made him richer than any Rockefeller, Getty, or Kennedy. He is also believed to be $1 billion richer than the Texas entrepreneur, H. Ross Perot.

Sam Walton says he really doesn't know how rich he is and he doesn't really care. He still drives the back roads near Bentonville, (population 9,901), Arkansas, in a 1979 red-and-white Ford pickup with bird dogs at his side during quail season.

Sam is anything but retired, however, and he spends much of his time flying in, and sometimes piloting, one of five company planes to openings of new Wal-Mart stores. At store openings as well as executive meetings, Walton is known for hopping up on a chair and leading everyone in the Wal-Mart cheer: "Give me a *W*—give me an *A*—give me an *L*—louder!" The cheer exemplifies Sam's approach to life, which features being loyal, working hard, putting in long hours, getting ideas into the system from the bottom up, treating people right, cutting prices and margins to the bone, and sleeping well at night.

Sam's home in Bentonville would be a real letdown for any visitor expecting the ultimate in lifestyles of the rich and famous. If you drive out to the mailbox marked "Sam and Helen Walton," you'll find a rustic, modestly furnished ranch-type house set back in the woods with a pickup truck sitting in the carport and probably a muddy bird dog or two running about the yard.

When Sam goes down to the Wal-Mart store in town, he might ask the manager, "How are sales?" Then he'll get what he needs from the shelves and wait in line to pay just like anyone else.

Is it hard to believe he never takes liberties in his own store? The manager admits that if it's bird season and he's in a hurry, Walton might just put down a five-dollar bill and tell the clerk, "I've gotta run. Would you take care of it for me?"

Tsk, tsk—millionaires can certainly be overbearing at times! As another example of how "overbearing" he can be, one morning he, the richest man in America, forgot his wallet. He had just gotten a haircut, and his barber of twenty-five years, John Mayhall, said, "Forget it. Just take care of it next time."

Sam Walton replied, "No, I'll get it." And he went home, got his wallet, and came back to pay his bill.[1]

If you're looking for a role model who knows who he really is, Sam Walton will do. He isn't marinating in hype or his own press clippings. The man who just may be the richest American is a success, but his money really has little to do with it.

DO YOU APPRECIATE WHAT YOU REALLY HAVE?

One of our great sins, which we seldom even notice, is taking too much for granted. We tend to complain about little things and fail to recognize what we already have. I often ask seminar audiences, "How many of you in this room do not have a fatal illness? Please raise your hand."

Approximately 99.9 percent of the hands usually go up. If anyone does not raise a hand, I don't point that person out. What I'm trying to do is make everyone in the room aware that those with any degree of health at all are among the top five percent of the people on the face of the earth. If you are presently not experiencing a serious health problem, welcome to the 5 percent club! Approximately 95 percent of the earth's population is finding it a real challenge just to survive to age forty-five.

It's ironic that in America we seem to take health for granted. We act as though it is something owed to us, and we lament the high cost of health care or the horror stories that create malpractice suits.

I prefer feeling grateful to just wake up in the morning. My eyes flicker open, I see the ceiling, and I say, "Thank God for another day. Let's go!"

I like what my friend Zig Ziglar often says, "If you don't think it's a good day, just try missing one."

Another thing we take for granted and fail to develop is all that potential we discussed earlier. Throughout our lives, we use only a fraction of our thinking ability. We could without much difficulty learn five languages, memorize a set of encyclopedias, and complete the required courses of dozens of colleges.

Reputable scientists have confirmed that we are getting by on just a tiny percentage of our potential brain power. We do not lack the brains; we lack the brawn of a stronger will and a higher purpose. Many of us don't learn and accomplish more because we are too lazy to make the effort. It is easier to get by and make it to Friday and the weekend.

Many people say they believe that knowledge is power and that the best way to get a good job is to get a good education, but relatively few pursue that belief and turn it into reality. For most people, studying is like paying taxes or going to the dentist. It is something they do not like to do, and few will do it if it is not absolutely mandatory. Most people believe that graduation day from high school or college is the end of studying for life.

The United States has the most abundant supply of free educational materials in the world. Our libraries, colleges, and universities are bulging with enough data on every subject to make anyone who is willing to spend just one-half hour per night both intelligent and successful.

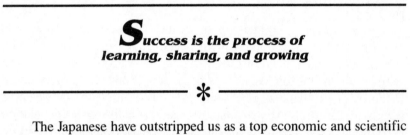

Success is the process of learning, sharing, and growing

The Japanese have outstripped us as a top economic and scientific nation primarily because they place a much higher priority on continuing education. They produce 95 percent of the TV sets we use to while away our hours in apathy and boredom.

We rested on our laurels, and Japan moved in. Now Japan is beginning to rest on her laurels, and guess who is waiting in the wings? China is starting to move. Chinese fifth graders spend a reported 114 minutes a day doing homework. Meanwhile, Americans average 46 minutes a day on any type of home study.

I'm never one for believing the myth that the good old days are gone forever. I much prefer preaching the gospel that the good old days are here and now. Nonetheless, we have lost something from the simpler times when athletes and entertainers were not paid astronomical sums to relieve our tensions, when kids did two or three hours of homework a day, when three of every four American workers weren't vulnerable to foreign competition. We remain the most powerful nation on earth, but we are no longer the leader in world trade. We trail the Pacific Basin and Europe, and we are not catching up.

According to a recent article in *Newsweek*,[2] we lack competitiveness as a nation. We simply aren't working hard enough, as proved by our growth and productivity of only 1.4 percent a year since 1950. This is

25 percent of the Japanese rate of growth and well behind that of West Germany or France. The critics say our problems are lethargy and complacency, with too much emphasis on perks and short-term profits at the expense of the long-term future.

Politicians are offering all kinds of solutions, multibillion dollar programs to retrain and retool society, but perhaps what we really need are fewer role models who seek $1.2 million a year to hit or throw a baseball, dribble or shoot a basketball, throw a football or chase down somebody who can. We just might profit from looking at someone like Warren Spahn, who played big league baseball until he was forty-four and, for most of his career, was to pitching what Michelangelo was to painting.

"BASEBALL . . . GAVE ME EVERYTHING"

Warren Spahn is a Hall of Famer, a winner of numerous awards, and rewriter of the record book for left-handed pitchers. He's a symbol of a simpler day when athletes gave loyalty to their team and not their agent, when athletes got high on victories instead of cocaine, and thought a $1,500 raise after an outstanding season was all they needed.

Today Warren Spahn runs the Diamond Star Ranch just outside Hartshorne, Oklahoma. He bought 50 acres in 1948, the year his then Milwaukee Braves won the National League pennant. Parcel by parcel he added to the property over the years until it now includes 2,800 acres of hay fields, pasture lands, ponds, and an oil well that generates $500 a month.

At the top of his game, Spahn took home a salary of $87,500. The average annual paycheck for a big league baseball player today is $412,520—and that's about triple the amount you'd expect in Spahn's day, even considering inflation.

Spahn never had an agent. He would negotiate his annual contract with John Quinn, the Braves' general manager, and even after seasons when Spahn would win over twenty games, Quinn would not offer any more money.

Spahn would say, "John, what do I have to do to get a raise?"

John would reply, "You're paid to win twenty."

When asked to speculate on what he'd be worth in today's free agent market, Spahn smiles and says he'd just like to be twenty-one again and have all his hair. He points out that he played until he was forty-four years old because "I was hungry. The desire was still there. Can you be hungry like that when you're a millionaire and your future is guaranteed?"

Spahn runs his ranch with the help of his son, Greg, an honors graduate of the University of Oklahoma and Spahn's only child. They are partners and good friends.

In addition to his work on the ranch, Spahn is in demand across the country as a speaker and does promotional work for the Equitable Assurance Company, AT&T, and Borden. He also plays in old-timers' baseball games, participates in the Fantasy Camp for Non-professionals held by the Dodgers, takes youth project assignments from the commissioner of baseball, appears in sporting events, and plays in celebrity golf tournaments. On occasion, he shows up at baseball-card-trading shows to sign autographs and talk about his favorite sport.

A widower for some years, Spahn lives alone in his comfortable three-bedroom ranch house, which also contains his office. He works at a metal desk and never turns on his telephone answering machine.

"Spahn Enterprises" has no staff, not even a part-time secretary and certainly not an agent. "Why hand it over to someone else if I can do it better myself?" he says.

Warren Spahn has fun traveling the country with his only message: discipline, hard work, and being willing to suffer can make you a winner. It made him winner of 363 major league games and of a battlefield commission earned at the battle for Remagen Bridge in World War II. He says, "I guess the secret is making the most of wherever you're at in life . . . I like where I've been and where I'm at. Baseball and the military did that for me. They gave me everything."[3]

ARE YOU LIVING AT THE RIGHT PACE FOR YOU?

One of the most meaningful relationships of my life was my friendship with the late Dr. Hans Selye. Dr. Selye, who died in 1982, is the acknowledged "father of stress." He began his research and writing on stress in the 1930s and gave the world his classic definition: "stress is the nonspecific response of the body to any demand made upon it." In other words, your body isn't particular. No matter what kind of pressure or excitement you undergo, your body responds by being stressed.

Dr. Selye believed that all of us have a stress savings account deposited in our bodies as our life-force. The object is to spend it wisely over the longest time span possible. The difference between our stress savings account and our normal bank account is that we cannot make deposits into our life-force or what Selye called adaptive energy. We can only make withdrawals.

People age at such different rates because some are big spenders of their adaptive energy account while others spend that energy more frugally. Well-known studies of Type A behavior in recent years dovetail with findings and opinions Dr. Selye voiced decades ago. But what do stress and Type A versus Type B behavior have to do with graciousness? A great deal, as we shall see.

The dangers of fast-paced, hard-driving, impatient Type A living became part of our vocabularies with the publishing of *Type A Behavior and Your Heart* in 1974 by Meyer Friedman and Ray Rosenman, two California cardiologists. Friedman and Rosenman had been researching Type A behavior and its connection to heart disease since the late 1950s when one of their secretaries mentioned that the chairs in the waiting room were getting worn down *only on the front*. Neither doctor was surprised. Many of their cardiac patients arrived exactly on time and wanted to leave as soon as possible. Those people literally went through life on the edge of their chairs, and waiting was difficult for them to tolerate.

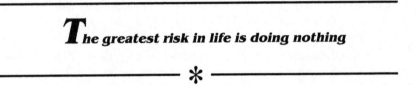

T he greatest risk in life is doing nothing

Friedman and Rosenman first called edge-of-the-chair behavior the hurry sickness but later dubbed it Type A behavior pattern. The Type A person is characterized by being ambitious, aggressive, competitive, and impatient. This person is tense and alert and reveals rapid and emphatic speech styles. Life is lived at an accelerated pace, and emotional responses often include irritation, increased hostility, and anger.

In contrast to the Type A, Rosenman and Friedman discovered the Type B, who is relaxed, easygoing, readily satisfied, and not as driven with the need to achieve and acquire. It would appear that when it comes to behavior and conserving adaptive energy, Type B is better than Type A.

Also tied in with Type A behavior in various studies is a cynical attitude, which is often displayed by people who are resentful, jealous, bitter, and suspicious. Still another attitude linked to Type A behavior is self-involvement. In one study of fifty-nine college students, the Type A's used twice as many self-references—*I, me, my,* and *mine*—with a correlating rise in blood pressure. Other studies have shown that along with feeling hostile and isolated, self-involved people have more second heart attacks.

Interestingly enough, controversy has arisen in the last few years about the connection between Type A behavior and heart disease. Some studies prove there is a direct connection while others show different findings.

Researchers working with Friedman and Rosenman find it laughable that the existence of Type A behavior is being challenged at all. The Type A behavior modification program being used at the Mount Zion Hospital and Medical Center in San Francisco has done a five-year study of patients who already had one heart attack. The results showed a marked decrease of recurring heart problems in patients who received counseling designed to change their Type A behavior.

Part of that counseling involves having eight to ten individuals meet regularly with a trained therapist in group therapy. One of the therapists comments, "Put ten Type A's in a room, all competing and interrupting one another, and they quickly begin to see how obnoxious this behavior really is."

The counseling zeroes in on four major kinds of behavior: anger, impatience, aggravation, and irritation. Patients do exercises to modify their behavior; for example, they may not wear a watch for a week, or they may be asked to stand in front of a mirror and smile a lot.

Type A behavior is not easily changed. If you suspect you are a Type A, you can probably confirm your suspicions by reading *Type A Behavior and Your Heart.* Chapter 7, "How to Tell a Type A from a Type B," will give you plenty of clues. For example, the Type A has a habit of explosively accentuating various key words while speaking. The Type A always moves, walks, and eats rapidly. The Type A often thinks of two or three things at once and almost always feels vaguely guilty if relaxing for even a short time.

Obviously, Type A behavior and graciousness do not make very good bedfellows. Aggressiveness, impatience, irritability, and anger do little to develop feelings of gratitude and appreciation for what life has brought you. One twenty-two year study has shown that aggressive children who become the class bully grow up to be less-successful adults, tend to hold lower-paying jobs, and often end up unemployed or in prison.

Said one psychology prof, "I think there's a very important message for parents: the traditional view that assertiveness and aggression leads to high achievement and success does not hold up under scrutiny."[4] In fact, aggressiveness can stack the deck against individuals. One statistical analysis in the research on childhood bullies showed they have a one in four chance of having a criminal record by age thirty.[5] This suggests repeating a myth and truth we looked at earlier:

Myth: GO FOR THE JUGULAR—WINNING IS WHAT COUNTS

Truth: IF YOU GO FOR THE JUGULAR, YOU CUT YOUR OWN THROAT

The Type A's of life stew in their own juices and do battle with themselves. To put it in Hans Selye's terms, our ancestors had an easier time of it. In simpler days, the appropriate response to a problem was fight or flight. Today with all our civilization and sophistication, there is nowhere to run and no one we can hit without regret. Most of us are caught in an invisible entrapment, which can lead to a host of stress-related diseases, including cardiac arrest.

Again, in Selye's terms, alarm and resistance—as a lifestyle—lead to early exhaustion. Emotionally upset, highly self-involved individuals literally withdraw all their energy bank accounts ahead of schedule, age prematurely, and run out of life too soon.

The Type B personality develops the graciousness that displaces the stress-filled life and replaces it with appreciation, gratitude, and that most uncommon component of all—contentment. To be the best you can be, Type B is definitely better than Type A!

DO YOU GO THAT EXTRA MILE—EVERY DAY?

In the provincial capital of British Columbia where the *Love Boat* stops in the summer filled with tourists who want to go back in time to the quaint traditions of England, there is a flurry of activity that seems to be at odds with the environment. After all, nothing is more important than afternoon tea at the Empress Hotel. Besides, it's been said that you can get arrested in Victoria just for walking too fast!

At first it looks like a typical Shell service station, but as you drive closer, you notice things—the sign, for instance. It doesn't just say "Shell" with the standard orange-and-black shield. The sign proudly announces "Dunsmuir Super Service," and owner Bob Dunsmuir isn't kidding.

You also notice cars lining up ahead of you, but you are willing to wait because you can tell people are being helped quickly and efficiently by a small army of young attendants who swarm over each vehicle like a pit crew at an Indianapolis 500 race. And when you get a taste of that full service at Dunsmuir Super Service, it's as though you have passed through a Star Trek time warp to find a new form of gracious life on another planet. You'll never return to self-service.

With smiles on their faces, attendants buzz about, pumping gas and checking oil and tires.

Oh, you can complain and tell them not to bother, and they'll cheerfully comply. After all, they aim to please. They just go right on with the rest of their regular service by asking you to step out of your car. If you're like me, you can recall being asked to step out of your car only by highway patrolmen or maybe cranky types who have no sense of humor if they get bumped from behind. Not quite sure of what's happening, you get out of your car and then stare dumbfounded as the attendants do the *inside* of your windows and finish up by vacuuming the front and back seats.

On one occasion a bus carrying an entire baseball team pulled into Dunsmuir Super Service for gas. The whole team got off while the Dusnmuir crew cleaned the inside of thirty-two windows and vacuumed the entire bus from one end to the other. If you leave your car for servicing, don't be surprised if you come back and find that they have also washed your car—at no charge.

These special touches are offered to everyone, no exceptions. And just for good measure, every Friday all drivers who buy gas or who have their cars serviced or washed are presented with a freshly cut carnation. It's spring every day at Dunsmuir Super Service. The little things really do mean a lot!

Another I-can't-believe-my-eyes feature is the station's outstanding repair and maintenance service. Not only are all the mechanics top craftsmen and honest to boot, but if your car won't start the next morning after Dunsmuir Super Service has worked on it, they send a tow truck to pick up your car. And on the back of every truck is a loaner car for you to drive during the day—at no charge. I've seen this done for special customers once or twice in Mercedes, Rolls Royce, or Cadillac dealerships, but I've never been offered a loaner by my local service station.

Station owner Bob Dunsmuir understands the power of graciousness and service. If you treat others the way you would love to be treated, you can't miss in business or in personal relationships over the long run. Dunsmuir has a unique recruiting philosophy. He looks strictly for winners. How does he attract them? Simple. He interviews job applicants *only* at seven o'clock sharp in the morning.

"That way," he reasons, "I see them before they get all gussied up, and if they show up bright-eyed and ready to go at seven, that's a good sign."

His attendants are mainly made up of young men and women going to college, trying to get into college, or on their way to a greater goal. Dunsmuir happily admits that his super service station is not only a place for a service station career, but is a staging area, a kind of career launching pad as well. Like most service station owners, he has a steady turnover in attendants, and that doesn't bother him. He says, "When these young adults come in for a job, I tell them, 'Look, you're just a winner in transit. The key is to be the best you can be at what you're doing. If you pump gas at Dunsmuir Super Service, you try to be the best gas pump jockey you can be. When you pump gas and give people service, you're giving them your value. Keep in mind that your next customer just might be your next employer.' "

And some of them are. His customers are the top people in the area, plus many visitors who come from far and wide to sample his nearly extinct brand of quality service. Bob has kept track, and he knows that dozens of young men and women who have served as attendants at his station have gone on to excellent positions in all fields of endeavor. Several are successful insurance executives, computer and office equipment sales reps, and service managers for large retail chain stores. You see, the people who get hired and advance the fastest are the ones who go that extra mile all the time—even when they're pumping gas or vacuuming cars.

A LITTLE DIFFERENCE MAKES THE BIG DIFFERENCE

I have always believed there is little difference between the top contributors and achievers in life and those who are frustrated and unsuccessful. But that little difference is whether the attitude is indifferent and negative or gracious and positive.

When Bob Dunsmuir took over that Shell station in Victoria, B.C., he did some thinking about the power of attitude. Instead of taking his customers' money for gas and hustling them out of the driveway as quickly as possible, why not give them the red-carpet treatment? Instead of going for volume, why not go for service and see if the volume won't take care of itself?

And that's what he did. Oh, yes, there was some extra cost—but mostly in effort, not overhead. Those little extras became standard: offering the smile, the courtesy, and the flower; vacuuming every car, front seat and back; providing loaner cars (not rentals); and doing decent repair work.

Instead of having a repair garage that rips customers off or gives them shoddy work, why not hire expert mechanics, pay them well so they stay, and give first-class, guaranteed work and that loaner car to drive free while you're doing it? After all, most people put off needed auto maintenance because they can't afford to be without their cars even for one day.

Dunsmuir's full service-superquality idea soon caught on, and customers began flocking in. Word-of-mouth advertising is not only inexpensive; it travels like wildfire. The Dunsmuir Super Service Station probably does 100 percent more business than the stations nearby, which have comparable locations, easy access, and the same caliber of gasoline in the pumps. But 100 percent more in revenues costs Dunsmuir no more than 10 percent above the cost of operating a no-frills station.

For final proof that his philosophy really works, Bob Dunsmuir recalls when he was seriously injured in a motorcycle accident in Boulder, Colorado. He had to spend a total of seven months recuperating in the hospital and at home. During that time, he had to trust the operation of his station to his mechanics and crew of young attendants. If you know anything about service stations and the way the help can dip into the till and sell parts to friends at "high discounts," you might think Bob Dunsmuir would have been headed for bankruptcy. But his training paid off. His young attendants didn't miss a dip stick, tire valve, windshield or window, inside or out. They ran the station as if Bob were there every day, with precision, grace, and efficiency.

Possibly even more significant, all his employees had access to his cash-flow records. They all knew exactly what his costs and normal revenues were. Even in his absence, the same honest philosophy was enforced.

During the entire seven months, there were no cash shortages, no dips in revenue, no missing tools or parts. The only thing that was missing was Bob Dunsmuir, but it didn't matter. He was there in spirit—a spirit of excellence, graciousness, and quality that money can never buy.

You can meet Canadians from Toronto or the remote reaches of Thunder Bay, Montreal or Medicine Hat. You can meet citizens from Vancouver and Victoria and more than a few Americans who might come across the border on business or pleasure. You can ask them if they've ever heard of Dunsmuir Super Service in Victoria. More often than not, you'll see eyes light up and smiles begin: "Of course! Isn't it the most incredible way to do business?"

I first heard of Bob Dunsmuir and his commitment to going the extra mile every day while listening to Bill Gibson, one of Canada's premier sales and marketing consultants and trainers. Bill and I conducted a seminar together in Vancouver, B.C., and I was impressed by his true story of Dunsmuir Super Service. As president of Newport Marketing and Communications, Inc., he uses Bob Dunsmuir as a prime example of how to do the best kind of sales training and customer service in the world.

It's funny. I went to Canada to teach a course on being the best, and I came home having learned how to be the best from Canadians who model it every day. I'm not surprised. I've never learned a thing while talking. I've learned nearly everything I know when I have seen and heard the truth.

Each person—Bob Dunsmuir, the service station owner; Warren Spahn, the baseball Hall of Famer; Sam Walton, the nation's richest man; and Graciela Gonzalez, the schoolteacher and mother—has discovered how to serve and to achieve in a uniquely different way. Yet all have the unmistakable, marvelous secret in common, the special quality, the one extra point that is the mark of a five-star person; they all believe it is more blessed to be gracious than to be grasping. Graciousness is the secret to being a five-star person.

HOW DO YOU MEASURE SUCCESS?

SUCCESS IS A very personal thing. It means something different to each of us. To 95 percent of the families on the earth, success is having some land to till, any job that pays, and a way to earn enough to provide nourishment for the children to grow in decent health into adulthood.

Success in America is usually associated with material wealth, fame, and social status. But I have been trying to illustrate in this book that it is not what you *get* that makes you successful, it is *what you are continuing to do with what you've got.*

Happiness and fulfillment seem to be associated with the richness of the experience in the journey, not in the fleeting moment of recognition of having arrived. You can't gain sucess and then sit back and enjoy it like a giant lollipop that never melts away. This is why the self-help myths leave us empty and hungry for the truth. Success is not a destination; it is a way to travel. As one of my seminar graduates put it, "The road to success is always under construction."

A feeling of inner joy and success seems much harder to acquire than a Mercedes, a stallion, or a castle with a wine cellar. To feel successful deep inside, we need to understand why we were created, who we are, and what we really want in life.

One wealthy, happy, and successful Manhattan real estate broker confided, "I could have made a lot more money in my life, but I preferred to sleep well at night." This broker found the ideal combination: outer as well as inner success, but only because he realized that all success must be built from the inside out.

Sleeping well after a good day at honest work is one of the joys of life. People who can't find peace in their own beds often seek it on the psychiatrist's couch. Psychiatrists grow rich counseling individuals who cannot enjoy what they've earned. People who seem to have everything continue to go from therapist to guru to cult hero to fad book and back to another therapist, trying to discover some joy in life. With all the outer trappings of success, they carry the heavy burden of emptiness.

People who play the comparison game immediately become vulnerable to feelings of frustration and unworthiness. When they see others who are smarter, younger, more clever, or better looking, the automatic conclusion is that the others are better than they are and the others deserve the best.

---

*R**eal success comes in small portions day by day*

✳

As we have learned, the success of others has little to do with personal success. True success is not measured by what others may say or accomplish. Though we all tend to compare ourselves with others, the happiest people in life know that they don't really compete against others. Their success comes from doing *their* best, based on their skills.

Instead of achieving or performing to impress the world or your peers, seek to do something that is beautiful, excellent, and heartwarming. Suppose, for example, you set out to learn to play a certain piece on the piano. You practice hard and long on the difficult concerto, and then you play it. You may play the piece one day for an audience of one or many, but that isn't why you seek to master it. You do it for the sheer exhilaration of doing your best. You need no one else to measure you or your skill. Your gallery is God and your own self-respect.

That's why it's so futile to seek success in one magnificent package perched at "the top." As we have seen in the story of Stripe and Yellow, nothing lasting or satisfying is up there. Real success comes in small portions day by day: a smile, a hug, a sunrise or sunset, sand between the toes, a satisfied customer, a child's happy squeal, the smell of lilacs, a hand extended, a phone call from a friend, a tree, a tasty meal eaten without haste. The list is endless, but our minutes to enjoy and appreciate life's small successes are not.

If there is one thing I want my children to learn from me, it is to take pleasure in life's daily little treasures. It is the most important thing I have discovered about measuring success.

The most important three words you can say to yourself: YES I CAN

---- ✳ ----

And, remember, it's not all that difficult to be a five-star person. Start with your God-given inner value, that's first. Add self-respect that comes from absolute and uncompromising integrity. Add purpose beyond yourself, next use discipline, and complete with the fifth rare star of graciousness, and you've got all five. Being the best is no more, and no less, than doing the best, giving the best, and being your best in everything you do.

The Reverend Charles Swindoll, one of the country's leading clergymen, sends the six thousand members of his Fullerton, California, church a weekly newsletter with a column appropriately entitled "Think It Over." A recent edition stressed the need to guard the heart from hypocrisy because its priceless treasures can be stolen if the head is turned by the so-called sweet smell of success. In that same column, Swindoll shared words by Ralph Waldo Emerson that beautifully capture the kernel of truth we have been looking for together. I have this same poem displayed on the wall above my desk, where I can contemplate it often. It is one of my favorites, and I hope you like it, too:

> How do you measure success?
> To laugh often and much;
> To win the respect of intelligent people
>   and the affection of children;
> To earn the appreciation of honest critics
>   and endure the betrayal of false friends;
> To appreciate beauty;

To find the best in others;
To leave the world a bit better,
    whether by a healthy child, a garden patch,
    a redeemed social condition, or a job well done;
To know even one other life has breathed easier
    because you have lived—
This is to have succeeded.

NOTES _____

Chapter One

1. Betty Cuniberti, "Yuppie Angst: Coping with Stress of Success," in *Los Angeles Times*, November 21, 1986.
2. Harold Kushner, *When All You've Ever Wanted Isn't Enough* (New York: Summit Books, a Division of Simon & Schuster, 1966), p. 16.
3. Trina Paulus, *Hope for the Flowers* (New York: Paulist Press, 1972).

Chapter Two

1. Denis Waitley, *Seeds of Greatness* (Old Tappan, N.J.: Revell, 1983), p. 140.
2. Philippians 4:8, italics mine.

Chapter Three

1. Jeffrey P. Davidson, "Integrity: The Vanishing Virtue," in *PMA Adviser*, vol. 5, no. 9, p. 1.
2. Ibid., p. 2.
3. Ibid., p. 3.
4. 1 Samuel 16:7.
5. Walter Shapiro, reported by Barrett Seaman and Laurence I. Barrett/Washington, with other bureaus, "Ethics: What's Wrong?" in *Time*, May 25, 1987, p. 17.
6. Material on cheating in high schools was gathered from a feature article in *San Diego Tribune*, November 24, 1986, p. 1 of the "Scene" Section, "Cheating: Just Part of the Game."

7. Quoted in *Seeds of Greatness,* taken from William Nichols, *A Treasury of Words to Live By* (New York: Simon & Schuster, 1947), p. 14.

Chapter Four

1. Barbara Schein's story was reported by the Associated Press and appeared in the *San Diego Union,* January 4, 1987, "Grandma, 50, Starts First Fulltime Job—Packing a Pistol, Wearing a Badge," p. A–28.

Chapter Five

1. Margaret E. Broadley, *Your Natural Gifts* (McLean, Va.: EPM Publications, 1972), pp. 3–9.
2. Richard Buck, "Are You A Square Peg In A Round Hole?" *Seattle Times,* July 26, 1983, p. D–1.
3. See Broadley, *Your Natural Gifts,* pp. 64, 65.
4. From Bulletin No. 121, Johnson O'Connor Research Foundation, Human Engineering Laboratory, Inc., 347 Beacon Street, Boston, Massachusetts 02116.
5. Gregory Jaynes, "In Florida: From Molars to Moonglow," *Time,* February 9, 1986, p. 12.
6. Adapted from verse by Waitley, Mullinnix, and McDonald appearing in *Goal Mind* seminar workbook (Denver, 1983). Author unknown.

Chapter Six

1. Suzanne Choney, "Creativity: We All Had It as Children; The Trick Is To Keep It Alive," *San Diego Union,* January 15, 1987, p. E–1.

Chapter Eight

1. I'm grateful to the Main Event Management Corporation of Sacramento, California, for providing the basic facts behind the story of the expression "under the gun." The story is supposed to be true, but details are sketchy. They have been embellished slightly for the sake of readability.
2. Philip B. Crosby, *Quality Is Free* (New York: New American Library, 1980), chapter 1.
3. Patrick L. Townsend with Joan E. Gebhardt, *Commit to Quality* (New York: John Wiley & Sons, 1986), p. xv.
4. From May 1986 *Reader's Digest,* large-type edition, p. 40, quoting Dorothy Heller in *Wall Street Journal.* Reprinted with permission of *Reader's Digest* and Dorothy Heller.

Chapter Nine

1. Adapted from verse by Waitley, Mullinnix, and McDonald appearing in *Goal Mind* seminar workbook (Denver, 1983). Author unknown.

Chapter Ten

1. Gerhard Gschwandtner's interview of Dr. Abraham Zaleznik appeared in the January–February 1984 issue of *Personal Selling Power*. It is reprinted in *Super Sellers: Portraits of Success from "Personal Selling Power"* by Gerhard Gschwandtner and Laura B. Gschwandtner (New York: AMACOM, American Management Association, 1986), pp. 8–18.
2. Information for the story of Domino's Pizza obtained from Jeffrey Zygmont, "Leadership Profile Series: Thomas S. Monaghan," *Sky* magazine, December 1986, p. 45.
3. For information on Martin Seligman's research, see Robert J. Trotter, "Stop Blaming Yourself," *Psychology Today,* February 1987, p. 31.
4. "Kill As Few Patients As Possible," *Los Angeles Times Magazine*, March 8, 1987, p. 4–B.
5. James Calano and Jeff Salzman, *Real World 101* (New York: Warner Books, 1984), see pp. 114–15.

Chapter Eleven

1. Art Harris, "The Richest Man in America," *Reader's Digest,* large-type edition, May 1986, p. 24, condensed from an article appearing in the *Washington Post*, November 17, 1985.
2. "The Quest for the '88 Issue" in *Newsweek,* January 19, 1987, p. 14.
3. David Lamb, "Symbol of Simpler Day: Spahn Gives Word Brave New Value," *Los Angeles Times,* February 21, 1987, p. 1.
4. See Meyer Friedman and Ray H. Rosenman, *Type A Behavior and Your Heart* (New York: Knopf, 1974); also available in paperback through Fawcett Publications, Inc., Greenwich, Connecticut. See also Joshua Fischman, "Type A on Trial," *Psychology Today,* February 1987, p. 42.
5. William C. Hidlay, "Bullying Doesn't Pay, 22-Year Study Finds," *San Diego Union,* March 8, 1987.

Denis Waitley has studied and counseled winners in every walk of life, from top executives of Fortune 500 companies to Super Bowl champions, from our astronauts to returning POW's. He is the author of "The Psychology of Winning," the premier audiocassette teaching series, listened to by more people than any other program of its kind. From 1980 through 1984, he served as a member of the United States Olympic Committee's Sports Medicine Council dedicated to performance enhancement of our Olympic athletes. He is a graduate of the United States Naval Academy at Annapolis and holds a doctoral degree in human behavior.